MW00488537

Hope for August

Hope for August

My Fertility Journey

Jennifer Kirsch

Published by Tablo

Copyright © Jennifer Kirsch 2020.
Published in 2020 by Tablo Publishing.

All rights reserved.

This book or any portion thereof may not be reproduced or used in any manner whatsoever without the express written permission of the author except for the use of brief quotations in a book review.

Publisher and wholesale enquiries: orders@tablo.io

20 21 22 23 LSC 10 9 8 7 6 5 4 3 2 1

Table of Contents

Acknowledgments

I wasn't sure when this book would ever come to fruition, as it arose from my simple daily journals. Those journals chronicled my most private thoughts, raw emotions, and crippling pain after an infertility diagnosis and the journey upon which I embarked to become a mom.

I began writing in 2015 what would develop into a manuscript, a manuscript that sat dormant on a flash drive for nearly three years. During late spring of 2020, I felt that it was time for me to finish it and share my story.

When I told friends and family members that I was writing a book, most of them had no idea of the genre or inspiration but offered encouragement. My intention was not to write the great American novel, as many assumed, but a memoir of the most difficult time in my life, a journey through loneliness and extreme shame. Perhaps it will offer some consolation to women who experience something similar.

To say that I couldn't have written this book without the support of others is not entirely true. This book would have been written regardless.

To say that I couldn't have survived the experience I went through without the support of others is unequivocally accurate. The word "thanks" does not begin to adequately express how I feel about my Inner Circle, colleagues who became my Protectors and lifelong friends, and medical teams Stateside and abroad.

To my Inner Circle (in no particular order): Tom, Gina and Paul, Beth, Teri, Brandon, Carl, Debbie, Megan, Rita, Diane, Heather, Cheryl, Vicki, Rosemary, and the late James Donnelly

To my Protectors: Doug and Rich

To my Parents: Paul and the late Patricia Kirsch

To my Writing Advisors: Anne Howley and Tom Purcell

To my Tattoo Artist: Jim Peticca

To my Cover Artist: Kameo Munnell

To the Staff at UPMC Magee's Center for Fertility and Reproductive Endocrinology, Dr. Robert Simmonds, and my doctors at Seasons

To Team Cancun: The Staff Fertility Center of Cancun, Jorge, Ricardo, and the Staff of the Ambiance Suites

To my Donor

The Moment That Changed Everything

We do not remember days,
We remember moments.

Cesare Pavese

Sleep was my adversary. I tossed and turned in bed in my home-away-from-home. Covers on, covers off, covers on. I fluffed my pillows. I adjusted the air conditioner from cooling to fan to cooling. In anxious anticipation I finally gave up trying to sleep at 4:23 a.m. I flipped through what few mindless English-language programs I could find on my otherwise Spanish-speaking television. I paced. I journaled. I sent emails. I prayed.

Around 8:00 a.m., I finally arose from bed for the day after over three hours of failed distractions to shower and prepare myself for the most significant day of my life. I'd waited nearly forty-five years and traveled over 2100 miles to arrive at this moment.

I put on a tribal print maxi sundress that would accommodate any residual bloating from the day's preparation and procedure. I took out my newly-purchased, intertwined heart necklace and fastened its clasp for luck and hope. This was a day of prohibited make-up, deodorant, lotion, and perfume. I was stripped down on a physical level. It paralleled my numerous months of stripped down emotions. This was a day of contemplating my darkest fears and having cautiously high hopes.

Just before 10:00, I walked downstairs to the hotel's restaurant for breakfast, as was recommended. The day required all of my physical, psychological, and emotional strength. My usual server had prepared me that Saturday was his day off. His second-in-command knew what I wanted for breakfast, as I'd become a regular at the hotel's restaurant in the days leading up to this. I choked down my eggs, fruit, and decaf coffee as my stomach anxiously churned. When I finished, I ambled back to my room to review my last-minute and post-procedure questions for my medical team. I sent and received a few text messages. Then, it was "show time."

I grabbed a bottle of water, my folder of pre-procedure instructions, and my purse. My palms were damp. I perspired lightly in the coolness of my room. I stepped into the hallway, alone for potentially the last time. I locked the door behind me and slowly walked to the hotel lobby.

Jorge, my driver for the past week, arrived at 11:15 a.m. The late morning Mexican air was already oppressively hot and heavy with humidity. It was stifling and difficult to breathe. We barely spoke on the drive. I focused on keeping breakfast in my stomach. Jorge dropped me off at the clinic on the morning of November 7, 2015. I registered at 11:30 and sat in the waiting room for a few minutes. Then, I was escorted to a pre-op patient room and changed into a scratchy, stiff, one-size-fits-most hospital gown. When I caught my reflection in the mirror, I openly laughed at the waif in the oversized gown looking back at me. Anyone else would have thought I was a little crazy. At least I still had my sense of humor.

Within minutes, the nurse brought in the final medical and legal release forms for me to sign and bottled water for me to drink. She'd return to collect the forms, answer any last-minute questions, and check on the status of my slowly-filling bladder.

I slugged cold water as I reviewed the paperwork. Everything appeared in order. Let's face it--I'd seen, revised, and approved emailed copies of the same paperwork weeks before. Despite all of the previously approved paperwork, the clinic needed my actual, not electronic, signature to proceed. I signed the official paperwork. Then, I sat alone for the next half an hour in my starkly-appointed pre-op room drinking the water the nurse brought me as well as my reserve bottle, painstakingly waiting for my bladder to fill.

I had no distractions. There were no magazines, Spanish-language or other, to leaf through. There was no television to provide white noise in the background. I was alone with my thoughts.

It was then that I realized the difference between being independent and being alone. I lived my life independently from my teenage years into my adulthood. I made my own decisions and abided by the consequences—good, bad, or indifferent. I traveled, unencumbered, when the mood struck. I took jobs and moved at various points. Essentially, my independent lifestyle allowed me to do what I wanted, when I wanted, and how I wanted. I lived on my own terms. While I was independent, I'd really never experienced true loneliness, the sense of having no one to support me, hold me, or sit quietly with me.

I'd made this trip independently and alone and was starting to reconsider that decision. That's when the loneliness intensified. No one was there to hold my hand or calm my excited, yet anxious, nerves. I tried unsuccessfully to meditate and set my intention for what I was about to undergo. I closed my eyes and breathed deeply in an attempt to calm my nerves. When that failed, I paced in my small room, partially to alleviate my nerves and partially to accommodate my slowly-filling bladder. I prayed that God would bless the doctor and his staff. I prayed that God would allow the procedure to be a success.

After downing a third bottle of water, when my bladder was finally full, I alerted the nurse. I'd waited all my life for this moment, and it was finally time. My nurse arrived with a wheelchair, and I moved myself into it, so my nurse could chauffeur me into a vast, sparse surgical room.

I lifted myself to the surgical table and asked for a blanket. When the nurse left for a few minutes, I took inventory of my surroundings. I felt like I was in a black-and-white movie; the room was void of color. There were sterile, medical instruments at the foot of the table, black-and-white, flat-screen monitors on the wall, and not much else. And it was cold--so very cold.

Then it truly hit me. The panic of being alone washed over me. My heart raced. My palms sweated more. I nauseously salivated. Was I having an anxiety attack? What if something went wrong? Only a handful of people even knew where I was, and they couldn't get to me if something went awry. No one, not even Jorge, was waiting on-site for an update on my condition. No one was waiting in the recovery room to sit with me while I rested. No one was back at my hotel to take care of me or lift anything heavier than my purse. No one was there to tell me things would be okay, that I would be okay. What was I thinking?

Just as I was about to move from the table to leave the surgical room, like there was anywhere for me to run, a second nurse entered for me to sign one last consent form. When she exited, Dr. Ortiz and my original nurse for the day entered.

I was prepped, feet put in stirrups, and told to relax. *Sure, I'll relax.* How do you relax when you're having a life-changing medical procedure done in a foreign country? How do you relax when your bladder is full, and someone presses an ultrasound wand on your abdomen? How do you relax when someone inserts a catheter through your cervix and into your uterus without numbing you? How do you relax when you're panicking and utterly alone? How do you relax when you know your life will be forever changed--regardless of the outcome of the procedure?

Despite my increasing panic, I focused on the ceiling and tried to fall into a pattern of deep breathing, but that was difficult because of the pressure on and inside my abdomen. I closed my eyes in an attempt to shut out Dr. Ortiz's Spanish instructions to my nurse. At that point, I just wanted it to be over.

I tried to remain physically relaxed through the discomfort and pressure. Imagine a painful Pap smear done through your cervix. There was a momentary pinch and a few minutes of pressure, both internal and external. Then, it was over.

I know the procedure took mere minutes, but it felt like eons. Dr. Ortiz moved to my left side and told me the transfer was complete. I was slightly shocked that the transfer was over in a significantly shorter time than it took me to fill my bladder.

Dr. Ortiz gently touched my left shoulder and pointed to the far wall of the surgical suite. I turned my attention to the monitors and really looked. It was right there on the monitor, the magnified pinprick of a white speck in a sea of blackness. There he was, my embryo, my future baby boy inside of me. The potential of his new life was inside of me. Was I already a mother? In a mere ten days, I would learn the outcome.

I don't know when I started to cry. At some point, I realized that my cheeks and chin were wet. That's when I felt tears slowly running down my cheeks. Dr. Ortiz touched my arm and told me everything went well; he told me not to cry. I explained as best I could that I was crying "happy tears." He left the surgical room as I continued to stare at the monitor.

My crying turned to weeping. I wept with joy and hope for the potential of my son and wept with sadness for the realization that no one was with me to share this miraculous moment--to see what I saw on that monitor.

My nurse resurfaced to wheel the surgical table and me back to my room to rest. She recommended that I not transfer from the surgical table to a gurney or the bed; rather, I should lie flat. After fifteen minutes of lying prone, my nurse returned to tell me to use the bathroom.

I have a teacher's bladder, but having a full bladder with people pushing on it from the inside and outside had done me in. I sighed with physical and emotional release as I voided my bladder. I returned to my resting spot on the surgical table and awaited the next phase of my protocol.

This time, it came in the form of hormones in a long needle that was administered intramuscularly in my upper right butt cheek. The medication burned as my nurse slowly depressed the plunger. I instantly bruised. It was by far the deepest and most painful shot I've ever had. It didn't matter if I stood, lay down, walked, or sat. The discomfort and bruising lingered for days.

I rested a while longer, then asked the nurse to call my driver while I dressed. It was time for me to leave the clinic. The rest was up to my body and my embryo. After all I had endured, I never could have imagined that I could have received the gift of life--and certainly not in this way. Just like that. In the matter of a few minutes, my life was forever changed regardless of the outcome. For the first time in the last eighteen months, I felt hopeful and cautiously optimistic.

I hoped and prayed for the best. I prepared for the worst. So the excruciating ten-day waiting period began.

A Lifelong Dream

**The joy in motherhood comes in moments.
There will be hard times and frustrating times, but amid the
challenges there are shining moments of joy and satisfaction.
M. Russell Ballard**

At this point, I think filling in some of my background is in order. Born in Pittsburgh in 1970, I was indeed a child of the Seventies, with the typical two parents and a sibling. I was raised in Green Tree, Pennsylvania, a bedroom suburb of the City of Pittsburgh, in the house where my parents still live. My father was the breadwinner, as my mom chose to resign her teaching position and be a stay-at-home mom after becoming pregnant with me. The majority of my friends' families were one-income families, so having one parent at home was the norm. Although we had one income, we wanted for nothing.

My parents--my mother in particular--exposed my sister and me to a variety of experiences. As a former music teacher, she always played music in the house. Whether it was records of orchestras or John Philip Sousa marches blaring to wake us on every patriotic holiday, we loved music. On random evenings, she would crank up the volume and let us dance ourselves into a frenzy around the living room in our underwear before bath time.

We were introduced to the arts at an early age. We visited the Carnegie Museums of Art and Natural History. We attended concerts and performances by the Pittsburgh Ballet Theater and community-based groups. We took instrumental music and dance lessons. Art supplies were readily available. One of my favorite artistic exploits was toe painting, not finger painting, in the driveway. We were given tempera paint and freezer paper and created our masterpieces. On those messy occasions, we were stripped down and had our preliminary "shower" in the back yard via sprinkler.

Summers were carefree--full of adventure and fun. We played softball and took swimming lessons. We hung out at Green Tree Swimming Pool most afternoons. We had our assigned chores and did schoolwork to prepare for the upcoming school year. We took walks at the local Nature Center. We made pilgrimages to the Strip District where we ate salt sticks from Pennsylvania Macaroni and drank Cherokee Red soda in the back of our full-size, green station wagon. We took weeklong vacations to Geneva-on-the-Lake in Ohio and long weekends at the Oglebay Resort in West Virginia.

I was creative, curious, smart, and sensitive. I knew right from wrong and how to speak up for myself and others. I knew, even at that young age, that I had a bigger purpose in life. That purpose was to be a mom. Surprisingly it had nothing to do with traditional family values, gender stereotypes, or my Catholic upbringing. I knew instinctively that it was something I wanted--that I was destined to do.

As I grew, my mom instilled in us the value of being a family. She fostered our creativity and encouraged our independence. She taught us about personal responsibility and the importance of honesty. When I reflect on my upbringing now, I wish I could be half of the mother she was.

During junior high school, I began babysitting for neighborhood families. Although I don't want to brag, I was an excellent babysitter. I packed my blue backpack with crayons, markers, construction paper, pipe cleaners, safety scissors, color pages, and puppet-making supplies. When I babysat, the children in my care worked on projects. Some were seasonal projects like the red and green chains we used to decorate a number of mantels at Christmastime. Others involved creating puppets over several sessions and performing puppet shows for the parents. There was no doubt that I was good with children.

At Keystone Oaks High School, I took a variety of high-level, academically-challenging courses and elective courses that allowed me to explore my varied interests, including a two-year child care program where I had the chance to plan and teach lessons and present activities and games to preschool children. I was born to be a teacher in some capacity. Through this class, I realized that I had the skills to be a good mother.

Outside of school, I continued to babysit. I also assumed the role of a student dance teacher at the studio where I took classes during my junior and senior years of high school. I taught preschool-aged students in ballet, tap, and basic acrobatics.

Throughout high school, a number of girls became pregnant, and most chose to carry their pregnancies to term. While I wanted to be a mom and recognized that I had the fundamental skills to do so, I certainly didn't want to be one at such a young age. I couldn't support myself, much less a child, so there was no jealousy, just a gentle reminder that I would get to join the "mom club" when it was my time.

I graduated high school in June 1988 at the age of seventeen with no intention of immediately continuing my education. I wanted to live and work before deciding on my path. After a couple of weeks working at Parkway Center Mall I had an epiphany. I didn't want to work at the mall for the rest of my life. Retail sales work was not for me, so I applied to Carlow College in Pittsburgh and was accepted.

Not only was I accepted, but I was also given an academic scholarship. I enrolled part-time in the spring term of 1989. By the end of that first semester, I was hooked and changed my status to full-time. I commuted during my years at Carlow and was heavily involved in campus life.

Throughout college, I dated on and off. More often than not, my friends and I would go out in groups. As this was the pre-Internet dating world, neighbors and friends set me up on blind dates. Most of those blind dates were what I like to call "one and done"—one date and no more of that man. Sure there were a few guys I'd gone out with, but there wasn't anyone "special" to me. Some of my friends got engaged and a few had children. That reignited my desire to become a mother, but there was no sense of urgency.

By the time I graduated with bachelor's degrees in English and Writing in 1993, I'd traveled, for a second time, to Europe, staying with friends in Sweden and London. After graduation, I free-lanced at Black Box Corporation and MARC Advertising, with whom I'd interned during my final semester in college. I didn't have luck finding anything permanent in the advertising/public relations fields, so I returned to Carlow to pursue my teaching certificate.

At that point, I put my personal life on indefinite hold since I wasn't working and was attending classes full-time. I did date one man for a few months during that time, but then I began my student teaching, which was the equivalent of a forty-hour work week, two to three hours of work each night, and no income. That definitely threw a wrench into any semblance of a personal life. Still, I longed to find that man with whom I would fall in love and want to have a child.

I finished my teaching certification program and student teaching within the calendar year of 1994, and I spent the next two and a half years day-to-day subbing and filling short leaves of absence. I knew teachers had to pay their dues, and I certainly did. More friends married and had children. I continued to go on blind dates. No one clicked for me, so baby making was put on the back burner again. Since I was then in my mid-twenties, I thought there was no rush.

In August 1997, I was hired and signed a contract with the Warren County School District to teach seventh and eighth grade English and seventh grade Reading. Warren County is about 150 miles northeast of Pittsburgh, Pennsylvania and worlds apart. I'm a woman who thrives on the energy of the city and the cultural and sports opportunities of my hometown.

Warren was the antithesis of the life to which I was accustomed. To say it was culture shock was an understatement. I taught students who didn't have indoor plumbing. People hunted for food, not for sport. Everyone knew everyone and their business. "Where do you work? Where do you go to church?" were usually the first two questions asked of me. I was thrust into a geographical area where it began to snow in October and continued into May. Snow was measured in feet, not inches. Once the snow flew, people didn't travel because it wasn't safe to travel.

I went on one disastrous blind date in the three years I lived in Warren. I continued to be set up on blind dates when I visited or stayed in Pittsburgh. There wasn't a special man in my life at that point. It was as if my entire life was put on hold, save for gaining experience for my teaching career. The notion of becoming a mother had been pushed so far from my consciousness and reality at that point; my total focus was on finding a contracted teaching position in the Pittsburgh area.

In early June of 2000, I moved back to Pittsburgh with no intention of returning to Warren. If I had to hold down two or three part-time jobs, that was fine with me. I needed to be back in a more metropolitan setting. I began graduate school at Duquesne University in Pittsburgh and interviewed heavily in the Western Pennsylvania region. By the end of that summer, I had two graduate classes under my belt and accepted a junior high school teaching position with the North Hills School District. I found an apartment and a roommate, with whom I taught in my new job.

To expand my circle, I took a variety of community education classes through the Community College of Allegheny County's Community Education Department but didn't meet anyone of lasting interest. More friends married and expanded their families, and the feeling of having a baby gnawed at me again.

In the summer of 2011, I tried my hand at online dating. After my first couple of matches and first dates, it dissolved into a game for me. I kept what I called "The Binder," to document my online dating experiences. My friends and family members chuckled as I recounted my exploits. I dated nine men that summer. I met a few nice men, but I didn't feel chemistry with any of them. I met some men who wanted a physical relationship only. Overall, it was a bust.

Then, I began a series of failed short-term relationships resulting from recommendations and fix-ups from friends. Again, no one of lasting or quality status came into my life. At that point, I was in my early forties, and I realized my biological clock was really ticking. I needed to put forth effort to investigate my options in my quest to have a baby.

I yearned for my dream of motherhood to come to fruition. I wanted to have the physical experience of being pregnant and giving birth. I wanted to experience every milestone that a mother gets to experience—changing poopy diapers, watching my baby roll over, seeing the joy when my baby would discover his or her feet, the trial and error of trying solid food, holding my arms out for the first steps, and of course, hearing the name "Mommy."

I looked forward to everything motherhood required—midnight feedings, swaddling my baby, sleep deprivation, and that feeling of immediate, unconditional love for another. In my case, realizing my dream would be more complicated than most. I just didn't know how complicated.

I'm very much a "Type A" personality who thrives on organization, order, control, and rationality. I knew having a baby would forever change every aspect of my life. My needs would be secondary. As a result, when I seriously considered embarking on the journey to motherhood, I considered what I thought to be every possible part of my life. Professionally, I was at the top of my teaching career and excellent at what I did. I was financially responsible and secure, with my mortgage as my only outstanding debt. I calculated the financial expenses of raising a child, factoring in food, clothing, childcare, routine doctor's appointments, establishing a college fund, and day-to-day living expenses.

I'd traveled abroad numerous times. I was physically, mentally, and spiritually healthy. I had an extensive support system of family and friends, and I would come to learn much later that my support system extended to my colleagues as well. Legally, my estate was in order. It was the opportune time of my life to begin this journey.

I also considered the potential challenges. I was single, so I knew I would need to investigate alternative options to conceive a child. I was also over forty years old. Knowing that I was born with all of the eggs I would ever have was also a concern; older eggs presented potential genetic problems. Additionally, older mothers also had increased risks to their own health.

All things considered, I decided that this could be my time. At my annual visit with my gynecologist in 2013, I began the discussion about having a child on my own, as I wasn't in a committed relationship. Dr. Simmonds, my gynecologist of over two decades, told me that I was physically healthy but that my age was working against me.

I shelved this notion for another year hoping that my personal situation would be different. I shared my dream with very few people. I didn't need judgment or questions. I needed honest feedback from those who knew me well. For male perspective I spoke with my dearest, lifelong friend Tom about it, and he thought it was "my time." I also spoke with my friend Brandon about it. He had some initial questions and jokingly offered his "donation" as a good-looking, handsome, blue-eyed and--let's not forget--humble man.

In June of 2014, I revisited the conversation about motherhood with my gynecologist. With my "advancing age" and single status, he referred me to the Center for Fertility and Reproductive Endocrinology at Magee-Women's Hospital of UPMC. I made my appointment that day and met with Dr. Wakim, a fertility specialist the following week.

At my initial fertility consultation, Dr. Wakim reviewed my medical records and advised me to stop taking my birth control pills and wait for two menstrual cycles to pass before he would order any preliminary testing. My body needed to be hormone-free. It was a case of "hurry up and wait," a pervasive theme throughout my journey. However, I was ready and willing to take any and every necessary step to conceive a baby.

Little did I know how physically and emotionally challenging and draining an undertaking my journey would be.

Options

When one door of happiness closes, another opens,
but often we look so long at the closed door
that we do not see the one that has been opened for us.
Helen Keller

Once I'd consulted with Dr. Wakim, I began a lengthy diagnostic process. At no time did I entertain the notion that I wouldn't be able to conceive a baby. It never entered my mind that there would be any obstacles that would preclude me from achieving my dream of becoming a mother other than my age. As I look back, I think the process was, in part, so lengthy to weed out women who weren't fully prepared for motherhood.

My diagnostic process began in in August of 2014 and ended in May 2015. In late August of 2014, I had my second cycle post-birth control period and made my appointment for preliminary labs. I had blood work and the first of many transvaginal ultrasounds. I was upbeat and optimistic about the test results. To me, there was no reason to think otherwise.

Let's face it--throughout my adult life, I'd taken excellent physical care of myself. I took a variety of dance classes, ranging from ballet to tap to pole dancing, and performed in a number of shows. I purchased and routinely did DVD exercise programs. I walked outside when the weather cooperated and did a short stint at my local recreation center's gym. I took Kundalini yoga classes, which balanced my body, mind, and spirit. I cooked the majority of my food from scratch, rarely eating fried foods. I drank socially. I didn't use recreational drugs. I attended church regularly. I had even begun a serious relationship with a man with whom I would later have a short-term engagement. I was healthy, fit, and was in the right mindset to embark on this journey.

Despite my optimism, my world came crashing down for the first time before work on Monday, September 8, 2014. When my then boyfriend and I went for my follow-up lab appointment with Dr. Wakim, his resident had the dubious distinction of reviewing my preliminary lab report with us. She told us that my ovarian reserve was pretty much non-existent. She didn't elaborate or offer an explanation; rather, she escorted us into Dr. Wakim's office, turned back to the hallway, and shut the door behind her.

It was there that Dr. Wakim explained what low ovarian reserve meant. In layman's terms, it meant that my eggs were not viable. At my age, there weren't enough eggs, and those that were present weren't of quality. Dr. Wakim further explained that in my case, my eggs probably had never been viable. Essentially, it wouldn't have mattered if I were twenty-three or forty-three in my attempt to conceive a child. All those decades on birth control pills, pumping synthetic hormones into my body, were apparently unnecessary. In retrospect, I most likely never needed birth control, as it was highly unlikely that I could conceive a child.

Blindsided, we sat in total shock. We expected to be told to begin trying to have a baby. Neither of us expected this news. I wasn't capable of asking any questions, even those I had written on my notepad. In the haze of shock, Dr. Wakim told me that I could repeat the labs in another month, but the results would most likely not change. It was then that I was classified as an infertility patient.

For a moment, I regretted not having looked into having a child earlier in my life. Would I have done things differently in my personal life? Would I have pursued alternative routes to have a baby earlier? Would I have researched adoption options? There were no easy answers. With later reflection, I knew I couldn't change the past.

I experienced an immediate and overwhelming sense of shame and grief. While I was still in a state of shock, Dr. Wakim walked us to an empty consultation room. He told us to take, "as much time as we needed." I sat in a chair in front of a round table when my tears began. I broke down. Tears morphed into uncontrollable, unstoppable sobbing.

I stood as my boyfriend hugged and held me as the sobbing continued. If he'd not been there, I'd have collapsed onto the floor. (Throughout my journey, the tears continued to flow.) I don't know how long we were in that room, but I'm grateful that the staff gave us the privacy and respect we needed.

Eventually, I became lucid enough to wipe off the mascara trails that had run down my cheeks. After I regained my composure and gathered myself, we left the office. We walked to our cars and went our separate ways to work. I didn't know how I drove to work that day, let alone taught that afternoon. The day was a complete blur. I don't remember what I taught. I was in shock and numb.

Later that day my boyfriend called to check on me, and I told him that I needed time. I wanted, no--I *needed*--to be alone to process the news of the day. It would be too painful to see the look of hurt on his face and the pity in his eyes for me. That night, I couldn't and didn't eat dinner. I turned off my phone. I broke down again. I sobbed, snot running down my face, rocking in the fetal position for hours. When I tried to stand, my legs gave way, so I sobbed on the floor. At a point I don't recall, I crawled upstairs to my bedroom and wept until I passed out in bed.

The next morning, I peeled myself from my bed, showered, painted on my face, and drove to work. A colleague, who has become a true friend, Vicki, poked her head into my classroom before the day's classes began. She sensed something was wrong. She asked if I was okay, and I shook my head and started to cry. I whispered through my tears a quick version of the previous day's news. She hugged me. When she left my classroom, I gathered myself for the day. Later, she shared that she thought I was "sick." If only I was sick, I could do something about it. I pushed my emotions down and continued the day as if nothing was wrong. No one else at work knew about my diagnosis.

I gave an Oscar-worthy performance at work that week. Yes, I made it to work each day, but I was on autopilot. My days resembled someone watching a movie, except I was in the movie. I watched myself teaching from the outside. It didn't seem like me, like the life I'd expected or felt I deserved. To outsiders, my family, my Inner Circle, and my colleagues, I appeared perfectly normal.

No one knew the devastating news I'd received. No one knew the gut-wrenching emotions I was having. No one knew my private pain. No one knew my dream of becoming a mother was dying. No one knew the shame I felt. No one knew how less-than-a-woman I felt.

I isolated myself for the rest of that week. I refused to let my boyfriend see me. I didn't speak to my family about the diagnosis. I privately mourned the fact that I wouldn't be able to have a baby. I dreaded each evening's grief. The tears kept flowing. I screamed at God. My stomach wouldn't allow me to keep down solid food, so I sipped on ginger ale and pushed fluids as best I could. When I did sleep, it was fitful.

By the weekend, I allowed my boyfriend to come back into my world. He stayed with me, holding me as I continued to mourn the loss of my dream. A sense of shame evolved. I felt "less than." To the outside world, nothing about me had changed. Within me, nothing would ever be the same.

I was so ashamed that I didn't share my infertility diagnosis with my family and Inner Circle until nearly two weeks later. A large part of that was because of the pervasive feeling of shame and grief. Shame about my diagnosis is something with which I still struggle.

It came down to this. I didn't want people's pity. I wanted people's encouragement. I didn't want to feel isolated, but infertility is isolating. It's not an acceptable topic of conversation. I wanted people's support, understanding, and love. I didn't want judgment for my decisions. It wasn't in my general nature, but I learned that I needed to ask for support and help. Maybe that's one of the lessons I was supposed to learn.

Every time I thought I was finished crying, sobbing, or screaming, more intense emotional outbursts surfaced. The most incidental things sent my emotions into overdrive. It could have been a diaper commercial or children playing in a park. It was difficult to keep my emotions in check at work, and a time or two that first week I couldn't.

I am grateful that those who "caught" me in a flow of tears, closed my classroom door, and let me cry. Those who had the courage to stay within the closed room showed their support for the unknown that I was experiencing.

It was a challenge to go out in public, as I had such little control over my emotions. Bad times were when I'd see an infant being cradled, in a car seat, or propped up at a restaurant table. Worse times were when I saw pregnant women. Whether they were complete strangers passing me in a parking lot or grocery store or one of my many colleagues, I couldn't stand or handle being around them. The worst times were when friends, family, and colleagues announced their wives' or their own pregnancies. Pregnant women were everywhere. I couldn't escape them.

If they could get pregnant, why couldn't I? I felt jealousy toward pregnant women and their spouses and partners. Emotionally, I couldn't handle attending baby showers. I felt that other women weren't worthy of having a baby because I'd be as good if not a better mother. I felt, and still feel, angry at my body for not being able to conceive a child.

The struggle with shame was continuous. As my body didn't function the way I wanted it to, I felt it had betrayed me. Not being able to conceive a child broke my spirit. To not be able to experience conceiving and having my own child was devastating. Being a biological mother was something for which most women wish. I felt, and still sometimes feel, less than a woman.

Despite my initial infertility diagnosis, I opted to repeat the blood work after my next menstrual cycle. The results were indeed the same, but this time I was more prepared. At that follow-up appointment, I was composed enough to ask the questions on my notepad that I'd been unable to ask at the previous appointment. The most important question was, "Could I carry a child, even if I couldn't conceive one on my own?"

The answer was, "We'll have to do some more tests." Despite the devastation of September 8, 2014's news and the results of the repeated testing, there was a glimmer of hope for me to have a baby.

Immediately after this follow-up appointment my then boyfriend and I were taken into an exam room to meet with one of the Assisted Fertility Nurses, "Egg Ladies," as I'd eventually nickname them. We were presented two options: the Magee-Women's Hospital of UPMC Donor Egg Program and adoption. We found out that there was a lengthy process, which included a specific diagnostic protocol to determine my physical ability to carry a child through an Egg Donor program that Magee offered. We were given a folder that outlined the Egg Donor program, provided numerous articles and resources, and given a diagnostic protocol checklist. While I couldn't conceive a child, there was an option for me, providing I was physically able to carry a pregnancy.

After this consultation, my emotions were on the surface again. We were given a folder of information that contained various informative articles regarding adoption and egg donation programs. I couldn't make it through reading some of the articles. The information they contained made me feel even less of a woman, focusing on the failed female reproductive system. My feelings of shame returned with abandon. I dissolved into the then-familiar, uncontrollable sobbing. Many evenings, my wounded body and spirit overcame me. On those nights, I have little, and sometimes no recognition of how I got to bed. Some mornings, I'd wake up not knowing how I moved from the couch to the bed. After my several attempts to read the narratives in the folder, our focus shifted to the clinical information versus the human-interest information given about the Egg Donor program.

We learned that Egg Donor programs came in three incarnations: in-house, private agencies, and egg banks. The Center for Fertility and Reproductive Endocrinology at Magee-Women's Hospital of UPMC offered its own, in-house Egg Donor program, where it "recruited" and screened its own egg donors. The advantages of using Magee's in-house program were that potential donors were psychologically and medically screened as much as the recipients, they were local, which essentially cut out travel expenses, and the staff also knew the donors. The fact that my team would be responsible for matching me with a donor of similar education, physical attributes, and health alleviated many of my fears surrounding the egg donation process. The staff was quite discriminating with its potential donors.

Essentially, the UPMC Egg Donor program assisted couples who needed eggs and could provide their own sperm to conceive a child. Their program offered two options: Non-Shared and Shared. Non-Shared egg donation offered couples one egg donor for their exclusive use. In other words, the selected egg donor would provide eggs to only one designated couple. The benefit of this option was if a couple desired multiple embryos or siblings with the same genetic make-up, a couple could utilize frozen eggs from the same egg donor at a later time. The cost ran upward of $20,000 and had a lengthy wait time.

The Shared option paired two couples with one egg donor. One of the couples would be the primary recipient; the other would be the secondary recipient. The donor pool was smaller. The eggs harvested would be split between the two couples and was at a slightly lower cost and an even longer wait time than the non-shared option.

There was an option of recruiting our own egg donor which would involve us approaching family members or friends under thirty years old, in excellent health, who fit our "profile," a woman who would be willing to undergo the same type of diagnostic testing I'd undergone, be willing to sign away legal rights to her eggs, undergo weeks of hormone protocols, and have invasive procedures including egg retrieval. We would be responsible for any and all medical costs that her insurance wouldn't cover, including medications and related procedures.

The second option for donor eggs was private agencies. There were private agencies that offered a large donor selection and shorter wait time than Magee's in-house program. However, agencies had the highest financial obligation starting at $25,000 and rising to upward of $37,000. The high cost resulted from offering non-shared cycles and paying agency fees, legal fees, and travel expenses.

The third option was an egg bank. Egg banks offered a larger donor choice than in-house but not as vast as agencies. The treatment cycle and wait times were quicker and less complicated. Its cost was also the lowest at around $16,000. Egg banks used newer technology with limited history of successful pregnancies. Additionally, some egg banks offered two types of eggs: fresh and frozen.

Fresh donor eggs were taken from donors who were on a treatment cycle. There were many potential challenges with fresh donation including synchronizing my cycle with the donor's cycle, having a smaller donor pool, experiencing delays if in a shared cycle, and a higher cost. Frozen donor eggs provided recipients with no synchronization, a larger donor pool, fewer delays, and a lower cost.

None of these three donor egg options offered standardized genetic testing of donor eggs. While the Magee program thoroughly screened potential egg donors, donors could still omit or lie about pertinent background health information. Agencies and egg banks didn't seem to offer as stringent a screening process for potential egg donors. Despite that, the in-house egg donor program was a distinctly viable option-- really the only option at that point.

Adoption was the other option presented to us. Adoption came in many forms: domestic, foster care to adoption, and foreign. All required sometimes years of pre-screening including questionnaires, background checks, mounds of paperwork, home visits, and high financial costs.

The primary difference between an egg donor program and adoption was that adoption eventually ensured a child while the Egg Donor program could not. The Egg Donor program provided an opportunity for a woman to conceive a child, not a guarantee. Since I wanted the physical experience of giving birth to my own child, I opted for egg donation, knowing fully that there was no guarantee of conceiving a child.

Inequality

**There was nothing predictable in this life,
and very little that was fair.**

Sara Donati

After taking some time to truly process the diagnosis of infertility and the options presented to us, I did what I advise others not to do. I researched information on the Internet. While the Internet provided a wealth of information, not all of it was accurate or trustworthy. Despite rationally knowing this, I began a short, intense obsession with online fertility sites. Each day brought a new level of information overload and subsequent emotional strife. It got to the point where I had to stop. I had to trust my medical team and the information they had for me.

I realized that even in this modern day, there's a societal disconnect and an inequality where infertility in concerned. Infertility isn't a subject typically shared or broached in polite or even private conversation.

Consider the following scenario.

Two girlfriends meet for a drink at a local hot spot after work. With busy schedules they see each other every couple of months but talk and text more frequently. After hugging hello, they sidle up to the bar. The bartender takes their order as they chat.

"Hey, Jennifer. How are you?" asks one.

"Oh, you know, I just found out I'm barren."

What's the appropriate response to that? Shocked dead silence? Throwing back a drink and immediately ordering and downing another? Asking for the check and leaving? A hug? It doesn't get much more awkward.

Simply, infertility is not something that is openly discussed. It's also tremendously isolating. That's when I had the epiphany that if I'd had a diagnosis of a disease or chronic medical condition, it would be more acceptable than a diagnosis of infertility.

Please know that I am in no way minimizing a diagnosis of any disease or chronic condition. My mother was a cancer survivor. Several close friends and extended family members are cancer survivors. My father is diabetic. I have friends and colleagues with arthritis and high blood pressure.

To me there just seems to be an inequity of resources, medical interventions, and general compassion and understanding toward the diagnosis of infertility in comparison to the aforementioned diseases and chronic conditions.

However, diabetes and cancer often show observable physical signs. There can be significant weight loss, inability to heal from simple infections and wounds, and fatigue. Both are "acceptable" diseases. For many forms of cancer, there are proven medical, surgical, and radiological treatment protocols. For diabetics, there are nutrition, exercise, and treatment plans to follow. Those afflicted with arthritis and high blood pressure can manage their conditions with exercise and medication. There are experimental and research studies that receive federal and private funding. There are support groups for patients, families, and caregivers. There are charitable foundations that raise funds for research.

Friends, colleagues, and community organizations routinely support someone with a disease or other chronic condition. Whether it's brining in a meal, coordinating transportation to and from appointments, babysitting, or sponsoring a blood drive, people are wiling and able to step in to help not only the afflicted person but also the person's family. In most cases, an immediate support network forms.

Conversely, infertility rarely shows physical signs. Women suffering from infertility look just like everybody else. Other than some temporary changes during diagnostic protocols, infertility patients' physical changes are often negligible. There are few support groups because no one really wants to talk about infertility; I certainly didn't. There aren't well-known foundations to underwrite research studies delving into finding the causes of infertility. People don't fundraise for others to seek treatment. Other than creating a GoFundMe page, I've never seen publicity for a spaghetti dinner or other fundraiser to help a person or couple pay for Assisted Reproduction or infertility treatments.

Typically, insurance companies cover all or much of the diagnostic testing, surgical interventions, treatments, and medications for diseases and chronic conditions. Some insurance companies even provide coverage for complementary medicine such as acupuncture, pain management, nutritional counseling, and mental health support. The fact that insurance companies recognize and cover these types of medical problems further shows the inequity of infertility.

Many insurance companies don't provide any type of coverage for Assisted Reproduction. Those that do, like mine, cover a small lifetime amount ($5000), which barely covers testing and medications, and doesn't come close to the cost of In Vitro Fertilization (IVF) or other procedures. This miniscule coverage is limited to participating providers only, and the rest is out-of-pocket.

Is this fair? As someone who has been thrust into the realm of infertility, I say, "No, it is not fair." I didn't ask to be infertile, any more than my mom didn't ask for breast cancer. While insurance companies view infertility as a condition, they don't provide equitable resources to patients for testing and treatment comparable to that of other conditions.

Consider the amount of money companies put forth in advertising budgets for Erectile Dysfunction (ED) drugs. While I'm fairly certain that a man doesn't want to need to use an ED drug, he has a readily-available contingency of options available to him. By virtue that ED drugs are regularly advertised on television and in print, it is viewed as an "accepted" condition and immediately treatable.

Infertile women don't have the option for a similar contingency of drugs. Is it because there's little or no profit in developing drugs to help women? For those women who are brave enough to speak up and share their stories, there is still a stigmatic feeling. There's no societal equity or support.

The Diagnostic Dance

Sometimes things aren't clear right away.
That's where you need to be patient and persevere
and see where things lead.
Mary Pierce

This diagnostic protocol to determine if I could, in fact, carry a pregnancy was much more involved than I'd ever imagined. The Checklist we received from the Egg Ladies outlined what we needed to do to determine my eligibility for the Egg Donor program. There were a handful of tests for my boyfriend-turned fiancé and three times as many tests, exams, and consultations for me. As a Type A personality, I appreciated The Checklist.

Diagnostic components of The Checklist, in no particular order, included: laboratory testing (copious amounts of various blood work), medical clearance and paperwork from my Primary Care Physician, a comprehensive physical exam with a breast exam from the Center for Fertility and Reproductive Endocrinology, cervical cultures, pap smear, mammogram, counseling with a Social Worker through the Center for Fertility and Reproductive Endocrinology, consultation with Maternal-Fetal Medicine if over thirty-five years old, a Mock Cycle, a sonohysterogram, medical clearance with a specialist prior to treatment cycle, attendance at an IVF Orientation, and a consultation regarding genetics. Some of the tests were simple labs, and others were invasive. All took time.

As our first step in The Checklist, we had an initial meeting with one of the Egg Ladies to discuss each aspect of the Egg Donor program. Immediately following that meeting, we met with a Social Worker to determine if we were of the right frame of mind and committed to each other to embark in the Egg Donor program. We "passed" the social work evaluation. **Counseling with Social Worker—CHECK**

We attended an IVF Orientation in January 2014. However, the majority of information presented during this orientation didn't apply to me. The orientation presented IVF from all aspects: physical implications for the female, the male, egg donor, if applicable, and the sperm donor, if applicable, diagnostic testing for both female and male, medication protocols, a general procedural timeline, and financial considerations. I understand that anyone or any couple considering assisted fertility needed to have comprehensive information, but since I needed both an egg and sperm, very little applied to me. **IVF Orientation--CHECK**

Some of my previous gynecological tests from my annual exam could be used for The Checklist if they were within the six-month to a year period, respectively. Thankfully, no additional Pap Smear or mammogram were needed at that point. **Mammogram—CHECK; Cervical Cultures—CHECK; Pap Smear—CHECK**

I scheduled an appointment with my Primary Care Physician, only to find out that she'd left the practice. I was "assigned" to another physician who examined me according to the protocol set forth by my fertility team at Magee. Her only concern was my family history of breast cancer. She reminded me of the increased risk of breast abnormalities from increases in estrogen as part of the proposed fertility protocols. Ultimately, she signed off on my paperwork and wished me luck. **PCP Appointment—CHECK**

I met with the Physician's Assistant from the Center for Fertility and Reproductive Endocrinology on December 30, 2014. While I passed the physical portion of the exam, the Physician's Assistant felt something in my right breast for which she recommended further testing. The hormonal protocol of a Mock Cycle included estrogen, which can cause or increase breast irregularities. With a maternal family history of breast cancer, it was strongly suggested that prior to the start of an estrogen protocol, I should have another mammogram to rule out any potential breast lump before starting a Mock Cycle. **Physical from Fertility Office—CHECK**

That afternoon, I met with doctors from Maternal-Fetal Medicine. Because I was over forty, I was considered Advanced Maternal Age (AMA). In this consultation, all of the risks for potential mothers over forty were presented. There were risks of gestational diabetes, pre-eclampsia (high blood pressure), and a host of genetic abnormalities were discussed. I left feeling oh-so-good about myself. Even though I was otherwise healthy, my age was still a wildcard factor in my goal of carrying a pregnancy to term. **Maternal-Fetal Medicine Consultation—CHECK**

Due to an ongoing, unresolved dispute between my insurance company and the health system where I'd had decades of previous doctors' appointments, gynecological testing, and procedures, I scheduled a mammogram appointment for December 31, 2014 at an imaging facility new to me. As I was scheduled for a diagnostic mammogram, an on-site radiologist read my films immediately. At that time, it was determined that I needed a 3D mammogram, which was also done that day at the new imaging center. Because I had dense breast tissue, the radiologist couldn't adequately see everything she needed to see, so she erred on the side of caution. The radiologist recommended that I have a Bilateral Breast MRI to rule out any lumps or lesions.

After a week of phone calls to the fertility office, the imaging facility, and my insurance company, I was able to schedule the breast MRI. I went to yet another new facility for this test. January 14, 2015, was the day I had IV contrast pumped into my body. I lay face down while the MRI machine clunked around me. Ultimately, the breast MRI showed no masses or problems with either of my breasts. **Breast MRI and (Repeat) Mammogram—CHECK**

The weekend after my breast MRI results were reported, I ended my engagement with my fiancé. That didn't help my emotional state as I navigated The Checklist on my own, but I was too far into the process to not know if I'd be able to carry a child. I made plans to proceed with the balance of my testing with my medical team at the Center for Fertility and Reproductive Endocrinology.

Luckily, the Center's in-house lab began scheduling patients at 6:30 a.m., so I was able to schedule the majority of my tests as the first appointment of the day and still make it to work by 7:30. This made having blood work and ultrasounds convenient and allowed me to miss little work. I became accustomed to wearing long-sleeve shirts or sweaters to work to hide evidence of multitude of pinpricks and bruises from sometimes daily blood draws.

In late January of 2015, I was finally cleared to begin my Mock Cycle after my next period. A Mock Cycle entailed vaginally inserting estrogen pills two or three times a day to thicken my endometrial lining to see if it could hold an embryo. After the appropriate protocol was followed, blood work and a transvaginal ultrasound would be performed to determine hormone levels and uterine lining thickness.

After the first Mock Cycle, my blood work and ultrasound didn't show the necessary levels of hormones or uterine thickness, so Dr. Wakim ordered me to continue that protocol for a few more days.

I took a half day off for the repeat blood work and ultrasound. Pittsburgh was blanketed in snow in the overnight for this repeat test. My school district functioned on a two-hour delay that day, but my appointment was not delayed. I shoveled my steep driveway and cautiously made my way toward Magee. I slid down my even steeper hill and made it to a main road. Bad sign--the main road hadn't been touched. It took me forty-five minutes to pull into the parking garage at Magee that morning. The waiting room was filled with other women, some of whom I recognized as frequent fliers of the lab like me. Our collective appointment times were delayed because staff members were late due to the snow and poor road conditions.

By the time I left the office, I was on emotionally shaky ground. I was so tired of being a human pincushion, bled by my vampire ladies. As I exited the parking garage, I found the roads to be in no better condition, so I decided to stop at Panera Bread near the hospital until road conditions improved. As I pulled into a parking space, my school district notified me that school was canceled for the day. At least I wouldn't have to worry about rushing to get home, only to have to change clothes and go to work.

I ordered a pastry and a latte and sat at a window table. While I gazed at the gnarled traffic, I began to silently cry. I was frustrated that my body wasn't responding to the Mock Cycle the way Dr. Wakim or I had hoped. I was emotionally exhausted from all of the testing and from the recent breakup of my engagement.

Then, I heard a familiar voice. I turned toward the counter. A woman for whose family I babysat as a teenager was ordering a coffee. I gathered myself as best I could, wiped my tears, and walked up to say hello. She's a nurse at another hospital and was on her way to work. She asked if she could join me. I assented.

I returned to my table as she picked up her order. My tears began to flow again. She sat down and asked if I was okay. I briefly explained that I had some tests at Magee and was anxious about the results. She had no idea of the reason for or the depth of my sadness, but she sat with me for about fifteen minutes. She shared that she was now a grandmother and would be soon for a second time. I was happy for her, but her news unintentionally increased my sadness. Then, she headed to work. I sat for a while longer and realized that she was my angel that day. She had calmed me down enough for me to eventually drive home safely.

Later that day, one of the Egg Ladies called with the morning's lab results. The repeat set of lab results did not show any marked improvement. I was told to stop the estrogen, wait for my next cycle and call in for a repeat Mock Cycle protocol. Why wouldn't my body respond adequately to the estrogen? How much longer would I be a human chemistry experiment, pumping hormones into my body? All that I could do was cry as I shoveled the mounting snow.

Approximately a month later, after my next cycle, I began my second Mock Cycle, where I was prescribed high-dose estrogen to thicken my lining more effectively. In this cycle, I experienced PMS symptoms on steroids: extreme breast tenderness and enlargement, abdominal bloating, weight gain, acne flare-ups, loss of sleep, general irritability, and crying for no apparent reason. God bless everyone around me during that time. They had no idea why I had become such a short-tempered shrew. Thankfully, after the high-dose Mock Cycle, my blood work and ultrasound results showed that I could, indeed, carry a child.

Mock Cycle—CHECK

Now, I had to wait for my next period to have the final blood work and last of the invasive tests. The problem is that my body was so inundated with estrogen that I didn't have a period for 72 days. I was bloated, my clothes didn't fit, and I felt just plain ugly. I called the Egg Ladies for help. After consulting with Dr. Wakim, I was prescribed progesterone to jumpstart a period. I took progesterone pills for a short time, and my period started soon thereafter.

Once that period came, I scheduled my final round of tests. The amount of blood work was extensive and included Free T4, TSH, anti-thyroid antibodies (antithyroglobulin ab and antithyroid peroxidase ab) prolactin, rubella ab, varicella ab (chicken pox), CBC, basic metabolic/chemistry panel, lipid profile, blood type and Rh, and infectious disease labs (HIV I/II, Hep B Surf Ag, Hep B Total Core Ab, Hep C Ab, and RPR. In plain English, I was being tested for alphabet soup that included: blood type, thyroid, cholesterol, and white blood cells to rule out infection, hepatitis, and HIV.

Knowing the volume of blood that was required, I'd taken the entire day, of May 8, 2015 off of work. In the early morning, I went to Magee for fasting blood work. I was fine when the nurse began drawing the first vial of blood. When she switched out more vials, I began to get clammy and had trouble hearing her speaking to me. I looked at her as she changed to the third or fourth vial. I started to slide down in the chair and mumbled that I thought I was going to pass out. I began to see a white light in my peripheral vision, as she removed the needle from my arm. Another nurse held onto me as I slumped further down in the chair. A cold, wet washcloth was laid across the back of my neck, and I was lifted into a wheelchair.

After being wheeled into an exam room, I was transferred to the exam table with another cold, wet cloth draped over my eyes. A nurse stayed with me until my coloring returned and my vitals stabilized. I rested and sipped on ginger ale. Eventually, I sat up and ate a few graham crackers. When the nurses thought I was able to, they helped me stand. They told me to get something to eat from the cafeteria or café before my next test. I still don't know how many vials of blood were taken. In retrospect, I should've taken someone with me as a driver, but I was ashamed of having to go through more tests to tell or ask anyone.

I slowly ambled from the doctor's office down to the café in the hospital for solid food and more fluids before my last test. I picked at a blueberry bagel and alternately sipped on orange juice and decaf coffee. After about half an hour, I returned to the office for the dreaded sonohysterogram.

Dr. Wakim's Physician's Assistant, performed a preliminary transvaginal ultrasound. Once that was done, she inserted a catheter through my cervix, flooding my uterus with saline as she simultaneously performed an ultrasound. I felt uncomfortable pressure throughout my lower abdomen and immediate cramping. My uterus was checked for any physical abnormalities, like lesions or tumors. Thankfully, it was a relatively quick test, and Dr. Wakim read the results immediately. The results showed no abnormalities. I was good to be sent home--in an adult diaper. Saline that goes in must come out, right? Heating pad on my belly, I rested that afternoon, with significant cramping. **Blood Work—CHECK; Sonohysterogram—CHECK**

With all of my Checklist items CHECKED, I was physically cleared to move forward in the Egg Donor program. I could physically carry a pregnancy! That was the most amazing news I'd received in months. The news soon became bittersweet. **Cleared to Carry a Baby—CHECK!**

At that point, I shared with my Egg Ladies that I was no longer engaged. I was informed on May 13, 2015, that, because I was single, I was no longer eligible for the Egg Donor program. The fertility practice with which I was working, did not participate in Donor-Donor cases. As I needed both egg and sperm donors, I was no longer eligible to be a part of the Egg Donor program. After enduring months of tests, my dream was seemingly over. **Egg Donor program--INELIGIBLE**

One Last Option

I'm not brave;
It's just that all other choices have been thrown out the window.
Holly Goldberg Sloan

What I thought was my last obstacle occurred once I shared my single status with the Egg Ladies. I was told that UPMC Magee did not offer a Donor-Donor program. Apparently, a number of years ago, the Center for Fertility and Reproductive Endocrinology at Magee underwent an ethics review. It was determined at that time that a Donor-Donor program, where a couple needing both egg and sperm, was deemed unethical. Since I required both egg and sperm, falling into the Donor-Donor category, I was ineligible for continuation in the Egg Donor program. I was told that there was only one option left for me-- embryo donation.

Prior to May 2015, I had no idea embryo donation existed. I needed more information, and not information from the Internet. I made an appointment to meet with one of my Egg Ladies. Again, I was presented with an abundance of new information.

That Friday in May of 2015, I learned there was a difference between a biological and genetic child. Biological children were carried by a woman (mother), and genetic children were of the DNA of the egg and sperm donors. I also learned that if I chose to participate in an embryo donor program I would essentially be a gestational carrier or surrogate for my own biological child. I'd undergo the same physical changes that any pregnant woman would undergo; however, I would require pre-transfer medications to prepare my body to accept an embryo. I would also need additional hormonal medications to maintain a pregnancy beyond the first trimester.

During that appointment, I was given information about several embryo agencies. Some agencies consider embryo donation is referred to as "embryo adoption;" however, a person cannot legally adopt a child who hasn't been born yet. She cautioned me to do my own research on the various agencies, as they differed in mission and philosophy.

While my fertility practice at Magee did not recruit potential embryo donors like it did potential egg donors, I would have to find my own embryo. However, my fertility team would help to facilitate my pre-transfer protocol and be able to do the embryo transfer if the agency I selected would ship the embryo to them. Otherwise, I would have to travel to where the embryo was being stored for the embryo transfer.

Since this was a new world for me, I was overwhelmed with information. I asked if my fertility practice could put me into contact with another infertility patient who was going through the donor embryo process. I just wanted to talk to another woman to see what her experience was. After several weeks, one of my Egg Ladies informed me that due to HIPPA laws, she would not be able to make that connection for me. She encouraged me to seek out online forums.

I found some online forums and blogs, but the majority of the content was centered on couples seeking embryos, not single women. I felt alone in a sea of the unknown. It seemed hopeless that I would find anyone who was going through what I was going through.

In my research, I found that embryo agencies function similarly to adoption agencies, in that many of the requirements are the same. Several of these agencies are Christian-based organizations. Each agency had its own restrictions. Some agencies worked only with married, opposite-sex couples. Some agencies worked with opposite-sex couples, same-sex couples, and single women. Most required some type of home study, similar to those done in adoption cases. Some agencies require you to use one of their subsidiaries for a home study, double dipping in a manner of speaking. All agencies required volumes of paperwork. Some agencies received federal funding.

Most agencies were privately held and acted as embryo "brokers." Think of those agencies as online dating sites for embryos. A potential recipient pays a fee and fills out an online profile. The potential donor views, selects, and contacts the potential recipient. That starts the process for the embryo donation.

I had many concerns with the embryo donation process. After online contacts with several agencies, I found that I couldn't speak to an actual person at any of the agencies I contacted online with questions. That was a red flag for me. How could a medical agency not have anything but an online presence? There was limited medical background on the donors, with no guarantee that the online information was accurate. Many embryos were "leftovers" from IVF attempts, with a higher potential of genetic concerns. Many embryos resulted from donor egg or sperm, so there was less medical background information available to potential recipients. No genetic embryonic testing was required; therefore, there was no guarantee of the quality or genetic health of the embryos.

Again, I was on information overload. I did some additional online research, but I became disheartened at what limited information I found. While I didn't give up on having a child, it just seemed so impossible and unlikely that embryo donation would ever be a viable option for me, but it was the only option I had left.

The Gift of Hope

Hope is the moonlight filtering through the trees,
Hope is the silent prayer that we make in distress,
Hope is the promise that we make to ourselves,
Hope is the happiness that we visualize,
Hope is the horizon that we reach, if we try!
Balroop Singh

On August 14, 2015, my life shifted unexpectedly and dramatically. A friend, Rita, with whom I had confided my infertility journey, provided me with an amazing opportunity. She put me into contact with a woman who'd been going through infertility experiences. Rita connected the dots. I was so excited that another woman was willing to speak with me about infertility, perhaps offer some suggestions, or be able to answer some of my questions. I looked forward to speaking with someone who "knew."

I called this still unknown woman, the Donor, who was in Cancun, Mexico at the time. We spoke, and she told me that she and her husband heard my story from Rita and were willing to designate, essentially donate, their genetically healthy, five-day-old, male embryo to me if I wanted it. What?! I could barely respond. After a few closing pleasantries, our call ended.

All I hoped from that conversation was to hear another woman's journey and learn something from her. Never did I expect that kind of offer. We made plans to speak again a few days later. I was in shock at the idea that someone could have the capacity to consider offering me an embryo. How does a couple come to that decision without having met the other party? It was truly remarkable. The only catch was that I would have to travel to Cancun, Mexico, for the embryo transfer, if that's what I wanted.

I needed time to digest this most recent information. I knew I was physically able to carry a pregnancy. Could I really become a mom? Could this really happen? A flood of hopeful emotions surfaced. I cried hopeful tears. I formulated a laundry list of questions about Frozen Embryo Transfer (FET) and the clinic where I would ultimately travel. I kept the news to myself.

Later that day, the Donor emailed me the egg and sperm donors' profiles and medical histories. There was so much information to read. Comprehensive family medical histories were given. Educational background was provided. Photos of the egg donor were present. The egg donor was Russian, and the sperm donor was American. Both were physically healthy, educated, and gainfully employed, had no genetic issues, had children of their own, and gave the ultimate gift of themselves.

Then I saw the most incredible sight. There was also a picture of the five-day-old embryo created in August. It was nothing more than a pin prick on my computer screen. Genetic testing had been done, and it was deemed a healthy male, no indication of Down's Syndrome or other chromosomal abnormalities. At five days post-fertilization, the embryo had been frozen.

When we spoke again a few days later, I was given all of the information about the Fertility Clinic Cancun (FCC), where the Donor had her own embryo transfer. She gave me information on all of the ancillary things—personalities of the doctors and staff at FCC, the names of her medical tourism director and hotel, information about airline travel. You name it; she shared everything. That was a different kind of information overload.

After much thought, I contacted FCC directly. I had a lot of questions regarding FCC and the embryo transfer process. I spoke with Jennifer Furey, FCC's Patient Coordinator. She answered many of my questions, and I was given more information. I was advised to look at the clinic's web site and contact her with any further questions.

After speaking with Jennifer and doing my own research about FCC and FET, I decided to embrace the gift that had been presented to me.

It Was My Time

**I've definitely learned that if you really want something,
just go for it, no matter how much it scares you.**
Bethany Mota

Once I decided to move forward with the embryo transfer in late
August of 2015, my hyper-organizational skills kicked in, and I
proceeded with calculated precision, creating and maintaining my own
checklist, and keeping detailed notes of the process. There was a
plethora of paperwork including a medical history, a list of potential
additional tests, legal documents, financial obligations, medical
protocols, and a proposed timeline. Although some of the steps I
needed to take were time-consuming and had a certain amount of wait
time, the potential of being pregnant by Thanksgiving was a legitimate
possibility.

I was put into contact with Dr. Azul Torres (Dr. Azul), who oversaw
my medical protocol and became my primary medical contact person at
the Fertility Center of Cancun (FCC). I began to wade my way through
the extensive medical paperwork, which required coordination among
my fertility team at Magee, my OBGYN's office, and my new team
in Cancun. I filled out FCC's paperwork, which included a
comprehensive, multiple-page medical history. Since I'd had the lion's
share of the required blood work, tissue samples, and other related
diagnostic tests, I requested my medical files from my OBGYN and
fertility doctors' offices. Since it would take longer to have Magee send
me hard copies of my medical records, one of the secretaries copied
my records for me. She had them ready for me to physically pick
up early on a Saturday morning. She made sure I had all of my test
results, doctor's notes, and related reports. She definitely went above
and beyond what I expected.

I scanned and emailed over 150 pages of medical records for review by my new medical team in Cancun. I electronically corresponded with doctors and support staff at FCC on an almost daily basis to ensure my records were received and in order and to address any of my concerns as I navigated the process. Dr. Azul was prompt in replying to my numerous questions and concerns.

As my records were reviewed, a few additional tests were necessary, and a tentative timeline was discussed. My OBGYN was able to address a couple of issues regarding some of my previous gynecological test results. However, I was presented with a roadblock, as I attempted to have my Pittsburgh medical team at Magee work with me to coordinate these tests. Unfortunately, I was informed that since my fertility team at Magee was no longer treating me, they would no longer be able to help me. Additionally, my local pharmacy was not able to fill the prescriptions written by my team in Cancun as they were from a non-American licensed physician.

I panicked, as I was weeks away from the opportunity to attain my dream. I was also in a time crunch. I reached out to the Donor. She shared with me the name of an independent OBGYN practice in the Pittsburgh area that was ultimately able to help me. This independent practice could help coordinate and perform any additional diagnostic testing and could write prescriptions for medications for me as I had prescriptions from my medical team in Cancun.

In the interim, I met with one of the doctors at my new OBGYN practice to follow up on another matter. One of the doctors wrote prescriptions for the two hormone medications. I made appointments with the independent OBGYN practice for my final ultrasound and to administer a hormone shot once the time came.

Other than the copious amount of medical paperwork to review, fill out, and submit, I reviewed the legal documents associated with my embryo transfer. There was a standard contract that ensured the transfer of legal rights to the embryo from the Donor and her husband to me, the Recipient. The Donor and I spoke several times regarding the legal documents that had been emailed from FCC to both of us.

We agreed that there were some minor changes that needed to be made. We independently sent our changes to FCC, so that the appropriate revisions could be made. Once those revisions were incorporated into the legal paperwork, we both signed our respective copies and submitted them to FCC electronically.

Financially, there was paperwork to review as well. The cost of an FET at FCC was significantly less than in the States at a mere $2400, which included vitrification, or the frozen storage of the embryo. I was able to immediately cover the costs of the embryonic storage and transfer. Without getting into specifics of why, I had met with my financial planner earlier in the fall of 2015 to discuss the possibility of liquidating some of my assets to cover any additional expenses I might incur in the last phase of my journey. A small portion of my assets was indeed used for airfare, hotel, meals, holistic treatments, and my driver's services. Once the financial paperwork was reviewed and completed I wired money to FCC, so I could begin the pre-FET medical protocol. Then, I initiated the liquidation paperwork with my financial planner as previously discussed.

I was proactive with my insurance company to make sure that the prescriptions that should be covered under my policy would be covered. I learned that one of the medications, a shot that would effectively shut down my ovarian function, would need to be filled through a specialty pharmacy. I followed up with Walgreen's Specialty Pharmacy to ensure that the correct prescription would be filled and delivered to the correct doctor's office. It took almost two weeks of weekday calls to my insurance company and the specialty pharmacy to work out the details. Everything was in place a mere three days prior to the scheduled date of my injection.

I was in almost daily contact with my Cancun team to keep them abreast of what was happening. I was on track with the balance of my pre-FET protocol. Physically, medically, and financially, everything was falling into place.

I contacted the Donor, who runs a medical tourism business here in the States, to update her on my progress. She offered to make my travel arrangements, coordinate with a Cancun-based medical tourism company, and book my accommodations. By the end of that Monday evening, I had confirmation numbers for my airline tickets and hotel. Within three days, the medical tourism company director contacted me. I was thankful that those arrangements were made. Kris was a godsend.

With my travel dates and arrangements confirmed, I completed and submitted Family Medical Leave Act (FMLA) to my school district's Human Resources Department. I would miss seven days of work. Unfortunately, my school district denied my FMLA request, as it viewed FET or any Assisted Reproductive procedure as elective and would only grant me a five-day, short-term Paid Time Off (PTO) leave. I was required to file a written request to my School Board for two days of unpaid leave, pending medical excuses. Two of my union representatives accompanied me when I made a face-to-face appeal of the district's decision with the Human Resources Director. This was an undue, added stress to my situation.

I received little follow-up from my HR Director, and my next pay was docked for the two days of unpaid leave. My union representatives supported me in my effort to have those two days reinstated with pay. After my return from Cancun, I presented a medical excuse from FCC, my two unpaid days were converted to PTO days and my pay was reinstated.

By October 2015, after waiting for what seemed like an eternity, I began my final medical protocol prior to departing for Cancun. I began daily doses of estrogen, which were increased every four days until I reached the maximum prescribed dosage. My body went into hormonal overdrive with bloating, weight gain, and breast tenderness. I struggled to fit into my clothes and was uncomfortable in my own skin, but I kept the goal of a successful FET in mind.

I had a final early-morning ultrasound at the independent OBGYN practice, which required a half-day's absence from work. The earliest appointment did not allow me to get to work on time, as my early lab times at Magee had. Dr. Azul reviewed the ultrasound results and ordered me to return to the same office for my Lupron shot. This intramuscular shot was designed to shut down my ovarian function prior to the FET. With a long needle and deft technique, the nurse as gently as possible administered the shot. At that point, my body only had to respond to the shot.

Then it was time to share my news with my family, as it was a mere two weeks before I was to take the trip of a lifetime. On October 30, two days before I made the trek to Cancun, I told my team of teachers that I would be on a short medical leave through November 9. Nothing more was said, no intrusive questions were asked, and they respected my privacy.

It was time.

Team Cancun, Here I Come

Life is a gamble.
There are no sureties.
If you want something badly, you'd have to trust your heart and
your instincts and then take a leap of faith.
Alyssa Urbano

In preparation for my Frozen Embryo Transfer (FET) I assembled a group of people who I deemed, Team Cancun. Team Cancun consisted of medical professionals, support staff, hotel staff, and medical tourism professionals. After weeks of planning and preparation, I was excited to finally meet everyone in person.

I made arrangements with friends to take me to the airport and pick me up upon my return. I'd had a Reiki session and a massage to clear my body and mind in preparation for what was to come. To maintain communication while I was gone, I downloaded WhatsApp, an app that allows text messaging and mobile phone calls through Wi-Fi. I was set.

My friend, Teri, picked me up on the rainy, early morning of November 1, 2015. I was packed and ready to go when she arrived at my house. She stayed with me while I checked in my luggage, and she stayed in the airport until I cleared security.

I had an uneventful flight from Pittsburgh to Houston. In fact, no one sat in the two seats next to me, so I spread out as best I could and slept for most of the flight. I had a short layover in Houston before boarding the plane to Cancun. I sat in front of a fidgety toddler, who periodically kicked the back of my seat. Normally, I would have spoken to the child's parents about the disruption to my flight, but during this flight, I truly didn't mind my seat being jostled, as I'd hoped that I would soon be that parent with a mildly fidgety child on an airplane.

Upon arrival in Cancun, we passengers were herded like cattle from the airplane to the immigration line. We filled out our return paperwork, which we weren't told that we had to have readily available for the return flight. Nearly an hour into my wait in this line, Jorge Portilla, my driver, called me to let me know that he was waiting for me outside of the terminal. I chatted with a young couple from the Midwest who were attending a friend's destination wedding at one of the resorts. When they asked about the nature of my trip I simply told them it was for "medical reasons."

After another hour in line, it was finally my turn to have my paperwork processed. The immigration officer deemed my paperwork and passport were in order, and I was cleared to officially enter Mexico. I retrieved my luggage, which had been left unattended for the almost two and a half hours I was in the immigration line.

Jorge Portilla, from the medical tourism company Health Ambassadors, was my driver, security detail, interpreter, tour guide, and sounding board while I was in Cancun. This six-foot plus teddy bear of a man waited for me upon my arrival at the Cancun Airport. When I emerged from the terminal, I immediately saw him standing to the left of the exit doors. Then the heat and humidity hit me. The weather was the antithesis of my Pittsburgh standards for the first day of November. As Jorge shuttled me to my the Ambiance Suites, my home-away-from-home for the next nine days, he explained a little bit about the history of Cancun and gave me information about some of the places we passed, including the Fertility Center Cancun (FCC) and the largest shopping mall in Cancun, which was within walking distance of my hotel.

Jorge helped me check in and requested that I have a room away from the front, noisier street side of the hotel. His request was granted. He made arrangements for security to escort me to my room. He would return the next morning to take me to the first of my appointments.

A security guard took my luggage to my room. The guard explained as best as he could in English how the television worked before leaving. I thanked him, then took in my surroundings. I had a sizable room with a sitting area that overlooked the pool in which I wouldn't be allowed to swim. I had a bar-style kitchenette with a sink and refrigerator. My queen-sized bed, closet, and cupboards took up the majority of the room. I had a private bathroom which was larger than my own at home. I unpacked, called home to let family know I'd arrived, texted those who'd asked to be texted upon my arrival, and ventured downstairs for dinner.

The hotel's restaurant became my late evening spot. I wasn't keen on being out and about later in the evening, especially since I didn't speak the language. In fact, I was advised that I should stick close to the hotel in the evenings. I enjoyed what I hoped to be my last glass of wine for nine months and beyond. After dinner, I headed back to my room and prepared a few last-minute questions prior to ask at my first face-to-face appointment with Team Cancun.

Jorge drove me to and from appointments that week, took me to, of all places, Wal-Mart, and showed me where to exchange money. He was on-call for any transportation needs or to answer any questions I had. Jorge introduced me to the staff at FCC. He arranged for my laundry to be done during my stay. Jorge coordinated my acupuncture sessions with a local practitioner.

I met the staff at Fertility Center Cancun (FCC) the morning of November 2, 2015. I met Jennifer Furey, the Patient Coordinator, with whom I'd corresponded frequently over the last couple of months. She welcomed me with a smile and a hug. She helped me check in at registration.

I met Dr. Azul Torres, Dr. Azul to me, who had coordinated my pre-FET medical protocol. She had been responsible for sending prescriptions for my medications, shot, and final tests. She received and reviewed lab results and adjusted my medical protocol accordingly. After finally meeting these women who had helped me to coordinate the upcoming FET, I felt at ease.

I was taken to an examination room for my ultrasound. I met with Dr. Ortiz and his nurse. Dr. Ortiz performed a final ultrasound to determine if my body was fully ready for the FET. It was. Indeed it was.

I passed the three final criteria: my ovaries were shut down, my uterus had no signs of abnormalities, and most importantly, my uterine lining was at an appropriate and acceptable thickness. He then reviewed the FET procedure in detail.

I was given a medical protocol for the week that included continuing my estrogen therapy and introduced high-dose progesterone to further thicken my uterine lining for the FET. My pre-FET restrictions included no swimming or baths because the progesterone was administered vaginally and would be diluted by water, no sex from that point, maintain a normal body temperature without getting overheated, and to remain as stress-free as possible. At that point, I was set for my FET Saturday, November 7, 2015, at noon.

I was able to purchase the progesterone at FCC. Little did I know that the progesterone I was prescribed contained peanut oil, to which I'm allergic, as a means of delivering the medication.

After my appointment, Jorge drove me to Wal-Mart to pick up a few essentials and food items for the start of the week. Despite my proactive phone conversation with my credit card company to let them know I'd be traveling abroad, my credit card was declined. Thankfully, my regular bank debit card worked. Then, Jorge took me to a kiosk to exchange money. He also gave me a local mobile phone for my use in Cancun. Finally, I was dropped off at my hotel.

I spent most of that first afternoon rectifying the credit card situation. Apparently, the credit card company had me traveling December 1, not November 1. The change was made, so my credit card was re-activated--crisis averted. I later ventured out to the mall. Under different circumstances, I could have done a great deal of damage to my credit card. With 234+ stores, dozens of eateries, and a multi-screen movie theater, I had daily people-watching entertainment.

My days became routinely mundane. I set an alarm to take the day's first dose of medications at 6:00. Then, I'd fall back to sleep. I struggled to wake for the day by 9:00 most mornings. I attributed that to the high-dose progesterone, 800 mg per day, I was prescribed. Other than one British television channel with all of its programs in English, I watched a channel that showed episodes of *Seinfeld*, as I began to slowly move about my hotel room.

I'd shower and get dressed before heading to the hotel restaurant for my breakfast. I had a choice of scrambled eggs or an omelet, refried beans with tortilla chips, fruit or orange juice, and coffee or tea. The wait staff pleasantly interacted with me each morning.

I cannot say enough about my hotel staff at the Ambiance Suites Cancun. My downtown hotel was in close proximity to FCC and the shopping mall. The front desk staff welcomed me every time I returned to the property. The housekeeping staff was amazing, keeping my room clean. My housekeeper even made animals out of towels and washcloths to brighten each day. The restaurant staff knew what I wanted each day for breakfast and always greeted me in Spanish and English. When I returned for dinner, they treated me kindly. The quality of the food was amazing. I still crave the shrimp tacos drizzled with chipotle cream.

On days I had medical or other appointments, Jorge picked me up. On the other days, I played "Frogger" as I crossed the main four-lane road in front of my hotel to walk to the mall. My second meds were taken at noon regardless of where I was. I'd spend three or four hours walking around the mall, people watching. Most of those days, I'd grab lunch at one of the restaurants. By 5:00, I'd head back to the hotel.

The balance of my afternoons was filled with reading online novels, watching concerts and movies, and napping when my body needed the extra rest. In the early evenings, I'd sit by the pool to write. On one occasion, I sat with my feet in the pool. It was the only time I was actually in the pool. My third dose of meds was taken at 6:00 p.m. After writing for a couple of hours, I went to dinner in the hotel restaurant. I tried almost every entrée on the limited dinner menu. I supped on tortilla soup, chicken parmesan, hamburgers, broiled fish, and shrimp tacos (mostly the shrimp tacos).

I was increasingly more tired, and my body underwent noticeable physical changes as the week progressed. My abdomen became slightly more pronounced, and my breasts were tender and larger. I guess that was a "silver lining" side effect of the progesterone.

I continued to lose track of time as my body slowed down and was forced to rest from the high doses of progesterone and continued estrogen. I had an increasingly ticklish cough and nasal congestion, which I chalked up to airplane air and the change in climate. One day morphed into the next. I texted friends and colleagues through WhatsApp. Quite simply, I was bored. Jorge checked in with me periodically.

Although I was around people all of the time, I was undoubtedly alone. I'd chosen to travel this last part of my journey toward motherhood independently, but it was definitely the one time in my life I felt a sense of loneliness, and perhaps a tinge of sadness, when traveling. Prior to this trip, I'd traveled abroad mostly on my own. Sure, I'd stay with friends along my past trips, so I had a safety net. I always maintained my independence, though. I had an agenda of places and things I wanted to see in any country I'd been. I enjoyed the adventure of the people I'd encounter and unexpected places I'd discover. I could eat my way through multiple cuisines on any given day. I could participate in events of a city or fade into the background.

This trip differed for many reasons. Outdoor excursions were off the table, due to the physical restrictions I was under. I couldn't sightsee, visit the Mayan Ruins, or embark on any daytime excursions. It was too hot outside for me. I couldn't snorkel in the ocean. I didn't even see a beach except when flying over one. There was no tasting of local specialty beverages. Even if I'd not had the physical restrictions, I was uncharacteristically tired. I didn't meet any particularly interesting people, except Jorge and Ricardo.

On November 6, Jorge drove me to my acupuncture appointment with Ricardo Pincilotti. It was a surreal experience for me. In the weeks before my arrival in Cancun, I'd dreamt of Ricardo's office. I just didn't know that it was his office. I felt like I'd been there before and described in detail the ascending staircase to his treatment room. The treatment room was as I'd pictured it in my dream. I had an unexplainable sense of connection and immediate trust with Ricardo. I was meant to work with him.

I'd had traditional needle acupuncture in the States before. Ricardo's method was laser acupuncture. The laser was directed to pressure points and meridians to improve blood flow to my uterus and to calm my central nervous system prior to the FET. When he was finished with our session, I was in a Zen state. He read my energy and noted that my energy was in balance. I was open and strong. At that point, I'd done everything physically and emotionally to prepare myself for the FET the next day. Everyone was optimistic.

That night, I researched types of progesterone I could purchase in the States. That's when I discovered that most encapsulated progesterone in mixed with peanut oil as its delivery system. That explained the mild to moderate anaphylactic reaction I was having with the persistent cough and congestion. I stopped the progesterone one dose shy of the FET.

I tossed and turned that night in anxious anticipation of the FET. I awoke, showered, and headed to the restaurant for my "usual" breakfast. Jorge picked me up after 11:00 a.m. I wore my good luck charm, a simple necklace with two hearts, one inside the other--the larger one representing me, the smaller one the embryo. When I saw it, I knew that it symbolized my baby and me.

When I arrived at FCC, I met with the nurse. I informed her of my concern and allergic reaction to the peanut oil in the progesterone I'd been prescribed. Dr. Ortiz confirmed that peanut oil was indeed an ingredient in the mediation. I requested a different form of progesterone post-FET in Cancun and for continued use at home. My request involved a long-lasting intramuscular shot of progesterone that would "cover me" with enough progesterone until I started a different kind of progesterone back in the States.

A Frozen Embryo Transfer involved thawing the designated embryo immediately prior to the transfer. The embryo would be transferred via a catheter fed through my cervix into my uterus. A full bladder was necessary for the transfer, so I was advised to begin drinking water upon my arrival at FCC, as the embryo was in the thawing process. That ensured that my bladder would be full by the time the embryo completed the thawing process and was evaluated for viability. If I came to the clinic with an already full bladder and had to void it, I would have to start drinking water all over again. I drank and drank and drank and asked for another bottle of water, explaining that I had a "teacher's bladder." Once my bladder was sufficiently full, I summoned my nurse.

I was wheeled into a surgical suite. I transferred myself to the surgical table. Two black-and-white monitors were available for my viewing pleasure. Dr. Ortiz brought in a picture of the thawed embryo for me to see. My legs were lifted into stirrups. Dr. Ortiz cleaned my cervix and inserted a catheter to make sure my cervix was ready for the transfer. At the same time, the nurse was pressing on my abdomen with an ultrasound wand. Full bladder, ultrasound pressing on full bladder, catheter in cervix did not make for a comfortable procedure. I was told to relax. Easier said than done.

Then, Dr. Ortiz fed the embryo through the catheter. I watched the entire procedure on one of the monitors. When he was finished, he spoke with me. I was in tears--"happy tears" I assured him. I stared at the monitor, looking at my August Embryo inside of me. I was overcome with emotion. In my mind, at that moment, I was a mother. I continued to weep happily.

I was wheeled on the surgical table back into my room. I lay flat for fifteen minutes before I was permitted to void my bladder. Then, I was given my intramuscular progesterone shot. This shot hurt worse than the progesterone shot that shut down my ovaries nearly a month before. I lay there for a while longer.

When I was ready, I got dressed and asked my nurse to call Jorge to pick me up. Jorge drove me to Ricardo's house for my second acupuncture session. Ricardo worked on me for about an hour to ensure blood flow continued to be increased to my uterus. Despite some periodic coughing during the session, I was able to relax. I felt so positive after this session.

That afternoon, when I returned to my hotel, I ordered room service and lay down. I napped on and off that afternoon. I reacted to any abdominal sensation I had for the balance of that first day. I felt my lunch digest. I thought I felt "fluttering." I tried to stay calm, all the while hoping my embryo was implanting itself into my uterine lining.

Post-FET, I was supposed to lie down and rest as much as possible. I wasn't allowed to lift anything more than ten pounds for up to twelve weeks, pending a beta pregnancy test. I was to minimize stress. I was to get as much rest as possible. I was not to swim, take a bath, or have sex for ten to fourteen days. I was to continue my estrogen and begin my new progesterone protocol as soon as I returned home.

On my last full day at the hotel, my rest was disrupted as loud music blared from the room below mine. I inquired at the front desk before I ventured out to exchange money before my return trip to the States. It seemed that a Christian-based church rented out the conference room directly below my room to hold weekly Sunday services. The music was music of praise. There was no better room I could have asked for, as prayerful singing and celebration were going on right beneath my feet. I was destined to stay in that room.

On my last full day in Cancun, I only ventured out of my room to eat in the hotel restaurant and walk to the mall to exchange my money. I packed what I could ahead of time, so I wouldn't have to lift anything.

Early on the morning of November 9, I called for security to help me bring my luggage to the lobby. Considering that I'd undertaken this most important trip alone, I was taken care of respectfully, kindly, and compassionately for the nine days I resided in my temporary home. I checked out, and Jorge was there to shuttle me to the airport. He walked me into the terminal, pointed me toward the right line, and we said our good-byes. After checking in, I ate a quick breakfast before boarding my plane to Atlanta.

The flight from Cancun to Atlanta was uneventful. Upon arrival in Atlanta, I went through the automated immigration process. I claimed my luggage to transfer it to my connecting flight. I was just happy that Customs officials didn't stop me, as usually happens upon my return to the States. However, when I returned home to unpack my luggage, I realized that my lock had been opened and the Transportation Security Administration (TSA) had gone through my bag. They left me a standard notice that they'd done so.

Being a multitasker, I phoned the independent OBGYN practice from the Atlanta airport to ask if they would be able to fill my progesterone and perform my beta pregnancy test in ten days. I texted a picture of both prescriptions to the office. By the end of my lunch, the doctor's office called me to tell me that they had already initiated the prescription process. As the first zone of passengers were boarding the plane for Pittsburgh, my neighborhood pharmacy called to let me know that they would have the first week of progesterone for me the following day, as it wasn't a regularly prescribed medication.

When I landed in Pittsburgh, my friend Brandon welcomed me home. He drove me home and took my luggage upstairs for me to unpack. Before leaving, he told me how much he hoped I would get the pregnancy result I wanted. I thanked him, and he left.

I ordered a pizza, as was my custom upon coming home from an international trip. I unpacked, showered, and fell into bed. Then the waiting began.

The Waiting Game

**The two hardest tests on the spiritual road are
the patience to wait for the right moment and
the courage not to be disappointed with what we encounter.**

Paulo Coelho

The next ten days were some of the longest and most exhausting days of my life. At work, I had this great secret from nearly everyone around me. It was difficult not to talk to my colleagues about having been out of the country and the purpose for which I was gone. I got into the habit of saying, "When I was out," or, "When I was on leave," rather than, "When I was in Cancun."

At home, I tried to resume life as best I could. It was difficult because I was anxious about my impending beta pregnancy test. I rested as much as possible. I continued to take my medication, which continued my increasing physical exhaustion. I was physically and emotionally wasted. I tried to keep my stress level as low as possible. Normally, to de-stress, I'd end my day with a relaxing, hot bath. That was indefinitely off-limits.

I observed more physical changes. I had more breast tenderness and abdominal bloating. I had "fluttering" in my abdomen. It was hard to focus at work. I was preoccupied and forgetful unless I wrote things down. I was so darn tired. My Inner Circle and female colleagues who were mothers took these as good signs. I believed in their good feelings.

November 17, 2015, was the morning of my beta pregnancy test. I was the first patient of the day at the independent OBGYN practice. The nurse who drew my blood said she'd try her best to give me a positive test result. The magic number was 5.0.

A beta pregnancy test, or hCG (Human Chorionic Gonadotropin) test, measures the amount of hCG in the blood. This hormone is present when an embryo has implanted in the uterus. It's made by cells formed in the placenta to nourish the embryo.

At approximately 11:00 a.m. on November 17, the wait was over. I called for my test results. The news I received was not what I'd anticipated, expected, or wanted.

The Aftermath

I don't know why they call it heartbreak.
It feels like every other part of my body is broken too.
Terri Guillemets

People say that without risk there is no reward. That's inspirational if the risk pays off. However, no one really considers or talks about what happens when taking a risk fails. I'd taken the ultimate risk in trying to become pregnant. I'd undergone months of lab work and invasive tests. I'd subjected my body to weeks of hormonal cocktails. I'd received disappointing news throughout the process. I carried the silent shame of infertility. I endured self-imposed isolation and the isolation of infertility. I traveled to another country for the chance to become pregnant with a baby boy.

I'd hoped and prayed for a positive pregnancy test, and I tried to prepare for no pregnancy. However, nothing prepared me in any way for what was to come. When I learned on November 17, 2015, that I was not pregnant, to say I was devastated is a colossal understatement. I'd thought September 8, 2014, when I was diagnosed with infertility, was the worst day of my life, but that day paled in comparison.

In times of a medical crisis, I have the capacity to flip into what I refer to as "crisis mode." It's a skill I acquired through my volunteer work with the Hillman Cancer Center and the University of Pittsburgh Cancer Institute. In my over eight years volunteering in Patient Care, I learned invaluable communication skills to help patients and family members understand and navigate the medical system into which they were thrust when diagnosed with cancer. I also learned that people want the simple dignity of someone to listen to them when they have concerns or questions about their medical care and bridge the gap between patient and doctor.

In daily life, these crisis mode skills have served me well. When a friend, family member, colleague or student knows of someone with a recent diagnosis of any illness, I calmly assess the situation and gather and process the information that's available. I focus on what the person needs to do to seek appropriate medical care, provide resources available to me and seek the help of others when I don't have enough information. I rationally proceed with what needs to be done to move the person on to the next step. I'm void of emotion until the person's needs are adequately addressed. Then, and only then, can I react emotionally.

I found that I was incapable of going into crisis mode this time. I barely comprehended that the nurse told me that my blood work revealed a 0 reading--no chance of pregnancy. I couldn't process that and went into a state of shock. My hands shook when I ended my phone call with the lab at the doctor's office.

No sooner did I hang up with the nurse, my phone rang. I thought that it must be the doctor's office calling me back to tell me they gave me the wrong or someone else's results. No, it wasn't the doctor's office. It was my friend, Brandon, the first person with whom I shared my news.

"Today's the day. Tell me something good, girl," he said in his usual, upbeat tone.

I struggled to steady my hands and my voice, "Zero."

I explained that I'd just hung up with the doctor's office and that I had nothing good to tell. There was no interpretation needed, as the minimum "magic number" for the pregnancy test was 5.0.

Brandon was silent for a few moments. Then, he expressed his sorrow and insisted that this wasn't the end of my trying to have a baby, that I had other options.

In my mind, I had no options. My goal was to be pregnant, and I wasn't. I didn't want to talk about "other options." I know now that he was grasping at what to say to me. As he continued to speak to me, tears began slowly streaming down my face. I couldn't let that happen. I didn't have the luxury of breaking down at work again.

Brandon asked if I could leave work and go home for the rest of the day. I told him that wasn't feasible. I had a tutoring program to go to a few minutes later and afternoon classes to teach. I whispered that I'd call him that evening, as my tears continued. Then, I hung up.

I emailed my team at Fertility Center Cancun to make sure they'd received the beta pregnancy test report and to ask if there was any chance the test could be wrong. Dr. Azul immediately replied that she'd received the report, and I was indeed not pregnant. There was no chance of a pregnancy with a 0 result. When I asked if I could stop taking my medications, she advised me that I could. She also expressed her regret to me.

I texted the handful of colleagues and my Inner Circle who knew I was awaiting news. As text replies flooded in, there was an immediate sentiment of disbelief, denial, and shared sorrow. I called my mother to let her know the test results. She was sad for me.

As the bell signaling the end of my lunch period rang, I looked in the mirror in my coat closet. The reflection that greeted me was a mess—puffy, red, tear-filled eyes, mascara running down my face, a blotchy complexion. I wiped the trails of mascara from my cheeks, blew my nose and walked, glassy-eyed, to the tutoring program. I was in a state of shock and numbness as I sat at a desk. I didn't speak.

When the bell rang again, I made my way to the computer lab, where my classes met that day. I can't say I taught. Rather, I oversaw my students in the computer lab for my two remaining afternoon classes. Thankfully, no students questioned my appearance or demeanor.

Throughout the rest of that ill-fated Tuesday, the few colleagues whom I'd texted, stopped by to check on me, offering a shoulder to cry on, well wishes, and prayers. When I look back at their reactions, they were in a state of disbelief as well.

At some point, my mother shared my news with my sister, who texted me to ask if I wanted to talk. She wanted to talk then? My reply was, "No." That was it. There was no other attempted contact from her.

When I left school at the end of the day, one of my trusted colleagues, Heather, stopped me on my way out to hug me. I stood stiffly while she hugged me, and I finally pushed her away. I couldn't look at her. I couldn't break into tears and try to drive.

When I arrived home to drop off my work and lunch bags, there was a voice mail message from one of my oldest and dearest friends, Beth. I returned her call simply telling her that I wasn't pregnant and had a therapy appointment to get to. She understood and promised to check in later in the week.

Ironically and perhaps luckily, I had scheduled an appointment with my therapist, Jim Donnelly, for the day of my pregnancy test. In retrospect, this was a godsend. I wept for more than the first half of our session. I think I used a box of tissues during that session. How was I going to get through the days and weeks to come? I hurt so deeply on every conceivable level.

Jim's advice was to first have a plan to address my physical needs and safety. Once those needs were met and I was ready, I could then turn my attention to navigating the grieving process. I needed to get nutrition, even though the thought of food didn't seem like an option. I promised to at least take in fluids. I needed to rest. My body needed to begin to process the fact it would no longer be on hormones and wasn't pregnant. I also needed to be in a safe space to begin processing my emotional reaction to the news of not being pregnant. Once I arrived at home, I would stay in for the evening.

By the time my session was over, I was talked out and more exhausted than I can remember being. When I got to my car, I texted Brandon to let him know that I was all "talked out." He replied that he understood. I drove home.

I began a period of self-imposed isolation. I turned off my mobile phone and didn't answer my landline. I ate a few spoonfuls of lentil soup. I fell into bed as I cried myself to sleep.

The next day was my forty-fifth birthday, but I wasn't in a celebratory mood. My colleague, Vicki, bought a birthday cake for me. She and Doug, another colleague, came into my classroom and sang "Happy

Birthday" to me. I began to cry as they sang. It seemed pointless to celebrate. For me, there was only loss.

I fought back tears all day. I knew I wouldn't be able to keep the cake down, so I shared the cake with my team of teachers. I sipped on peppermint tea and water during the day. I was too nauseous to eat.

Throughout the day, a few colleagues hugged or tried to hug me, but I pulled away in fear that I would start crying and not be able to stop. I couldn't stand to be touched. I physically hurt and being touched made my emotional pain seem too real.

A bright spot in an otherwise difficult day was when the birthday flowers my parents sent were delivered to my classroom. When I returned home from work, my neighbor brought birthday flowers that my friends Gina and Paul had delivered to my house earlier in the day. A handful of friends and extended family members texted and left voice mail messages wishing me happy birthday.

To the rest of the world, the day went on. To the rest of the world, nothing had happened. Life went on regardless of what I was going through.

Since it was an unusually warm November day, I took advantage of the mild weather. I raked and bagged leaves for hours. It felt good to do something mindless, monotonous and physical. I'd been on physical restriction for weeks. I worked until well after sundown. My next-door neighbor, Diane, checked on me as I worked, realizing I needed to do something productive while trying to process the previous day's news. She left her back yard lights on until I finished for the evening. By the time I was done, I'd filled thirteen paper bags with leaves.

I was actually a little hungry. I ate about half a bowl of the lentil soup from the previous night's dinner. I took a hot bath. I sat and cried in the bathtub until I realized I was shivering in the then cold water. Grief had taken over, and I sobbed myself to sleep.

Getting out of bed each morning became a struggle, but I felt like it was an accomplishment by not crawling back under the covers after my alarm clock rang. I'd wake in a puffy-eyed stupor. I let the shower beat down on my aching body until the water went cold. Although I didn't want to look in the mirror, I painted on my face, sometimes with three layers of under-eye concealer. I tried to eat breakfast, but more often than not, made and drank some juice laced with protein powder. Then it was off to work.

When I reflected on what my life had become, it wasn't surprising that some depression crept in. In less than a year's time, I began my journey toward motherhood, I'd fallen in love, ended an engagement, endured months of medical tests and procedures, taken numerous medications, been given the miraculous gift of an embryo, and lost my dream of becoming a mom.

On top of the emotional turmoil, my body began to exhibit unexpected physical symptoms. I suffered from night sweats for days, awaking in the middle of the night completely drenched and having to change my pajamas and sheets. Daytime sweats made me feel like I was having hot flashes. My body was riddled with flu-like achiness. Every part of my body hurt—joints, muscles, my skin and especially my heart. I had constant bouts of nausea, occasionally ending in vomiting and mostly ending with diarrhea. I lost nine pounds and looked peaked. Some nights I slept for a few hours--other nights barely at all.

Few things helped quell my physical symptoms. I didn't want to take anything for the nausea or achiness because I'd been on and off of medication for close to a year. Since food was not my friend, I continued to push fluids as much as I could to stay hydrated. I took nightly hot baths to ease my aching body. More often than not, I sobbed myself to disrupted sleep. Grief reigned supreme.

I continued to shut out those around me. I didn't return phone calls. I didn't reply to texts or email messages. I went to work and came home. I didn't socialize. I refused visitors.

I was short-tempered and irritable with colleagues and students at work. I couldn't concentrate on anything that required any sustained attention or focus. I forgot things unless they were written down or entered into my phone's calendar. I was prone to private emotional outbursts.

In the evenings, I dissolved into uncontrollable sobbing and rage. I pleaded with God. I screamed at Him.

"Why would you give me the gift of an embryo only to take the pregnancy away?"

"I want my son! I want my baby!"

"Why God? Why?"

"What can I do to have my baby back?"

"Why not me?"

God didn't answer and hasn't answered me.

After these anger-filled meltdowns, I rocked back and forth autistically in the fetal position with tears, and snot rolled down my face. I didn't even attempt to grab a tissue. Night after night, I crawled upstairs and into bed.

When my first post-FET period came within a week, I dissolved into tears again. Those were different tears, though. Having my period was the last physical sign that my dream of bearing that child was indeed over. That day things were indeed final.

Prior to my FET, my family and I had planned my annual birthday dinner for that evening. Although I didn't feel like eating or being remotely social, I dressed in my birthday finest and met them at the LeMont, one of my favorite restaurants. Pittsburgh's annual Light Up Night had been the night before, and our table overlooked the holiday-decorated downtown area known as The Point. Dinnertime conversation was forced, and I did eat dinner that night, my only meal of the day.

After dinner, my parents and my sister's family joined me at my house for gifts and cake. No gifts were necessary or could make up for the sense of loss I felt. It was hard to have people, even my family, in my space.

The conversation turned to planning the Thanksgiving menu. With the exception of two years over the last two decades, I host Thanksgiving dinner. At that point, I felt nothing for which to be thankful. With the stress I was under, my mother recognized that hosting dinner might be too much for me. She offered to host

Thanksgiving dinner. After thinking it over, I accepted her offer. That way, I could arrive and leave when I wanted. Each household would contribute to the meal.

In the meantime, my friend, Brandon, was one of the few brave souls to reach out to me. He called a week after I shared that I wasn't pregnant. He offered his own form of tough love. He wanted to fix the situation for me or at least help me to do so. He wanted to take away my pain. Knowing me well, he told me I needed a plan. Anyone who knew me knew I typically function in a rational state of mind and always have a back-up plan to each plan. He told me that my attempt to become a mother wasn't over, and I had other options. He told me to consider those options. He told me, told me, told me.

I didn't need to be "told" anything. All I could do was cry. I barely spoke. I needed compassion. Despite not wanting to be physically touched, I truly needed someone to hold me, crying and screaming, and tell me I would be okay, that the pain would go away.

I wasn't ready to look at any other options. I was mourning the failed FET and the death of my dream to bear a child and had unknowingly battled withdrawal. His intention came out of pure caring, but his execution sucked. I wasn't able to articulate these things to him, and I sobbed for nearly an hour after ending that phone call.

When Thanksgiving arrived that Thursday, I didn't feel like watching the Macy's Thanksgiving Day Parade, which was my tradition. It was a chore to pull myself together. I loaded my side dishes into my car and drove to my parents' house. I ate a small plateful of turkey and accompaniments, my sole meal of the day. Then I was ready to go home.

After nearly two weeks of feeling physically lousy, I looked online to try to figure out what these symptoms could mean. I was shocked to find repeated online sources state that I was experiencing withdrawal symptoms similar to those of someone who was withdrawing from benzodiazepines, anti-anxiety medications.

I contacted my team in Cancun to see if what I'd researched online was accurate. Dr. Azul verified that I was indeed in withdrawal, and

I should be nearing its end. By stopping the hormonal medications cold turkey, my body was thrown into full-scale withdrawal. At least I knew the cause of my physical symptoms and my irritability with those around me. I was angry that I was not weaned from the medications.

As my withdrawal symptoms dissipated, I began to reach out to family and friends. Some of them had texted or called me during my isolation whether I responded or not. All had offered support and respected my need for privacy.

When my withdrawal finally came to an end, Jim, my therapist, told me that the emotional work would begin. He told me that sometimes seemingly insignificant things might and probably would set me off. The only thing to do was to allow myself to feel what I was feeling. Then, I could start to process the emotions without judging them or myself. What had I been doing for the last two weeks? I did not look forward to more of that.

I also needed to begin the process of reclaiming my physical body. Once the nausea waned, I began to eat a little more. The addition of nutritious food helped my energy level. When the weather cooperated, I began to walk after work, since my body aches had disappeared. I even broke out an exercise DVD. Doing something physical seemed to make me feel better.

My therapist was correct about the end of my physical withdrawal. I began to experience every little emotion in a heightened state. For the most part, I fought to maintain my composure at work and in public. In private, I was a mess. There were days when I'd begin to cry on the drive home from work. I'd sit in my car, garage door down, engine off, shaking, crying, and screaming. Television commercials for diapers, children's toys and the like set me into a tearful tailspin.

For some reason, I remembered Elizabeth Kubler-Ross published *On Death and Dying*, which I'd studied in eighth grade Health class. I recalled her five stages of grief: Denial, Anger, Bargaining, Depression, and Acceptance (DABDA). Looking back, I went through some of those five stages.

My denial came in the form of questioning the beta pregnancy test results. The results must have been wrong; however, upon reflection, there was no changing a 0.0 test result.

I quickly moved into the anger phase. My daily bouts of crying turned to sobbing and screaming. I screamed primally to rid myself of the pain I felt. I raged at God until I was hoarse. I soaked numerous pillowcases and pillows with my tears. I fell into the fetal position in my kitchen, living room, bedroom, and bathtub. I bristled and tensed when someone tried to touch me.

Would my anguish ever end? Would I ever be happy again? Would I allow others to touch me again? What kind of God would present me with such an extraordinary series of events and opportunities only to take the end result away? My anger hasn't completely gone away.

My self-imposed isolation was coming to an end, but my general isolation continued. Jim warned me that I would notice that life for others would continue on, but I might feel that I was being left behind. I felt that during the holidays of 2015. It seemed like all those around me were moving on with their lives, celebrating, starting new relationships, and working--and I was stuck. He cautioned me that I might feel a degree of angst toward others for not understanding my emotional anguish, and that's exactly what happened.

I felt betrayed by those who started or continued new relationships, because I was left to deal with my loss without their support. I was left behind. I felt judged by others who chose not to support me at all. I felt misunderstood when I tried to share what I was experiencing. I felt like no one understood what I was going through. Anger continued to rear its head for weeks.

I can't say that I bargained with God or the universe. There was nothing for which to bargain.

Depression surfaced as I continued to struggle to get out of bed in the morning. I forced myself to rise, shower, and get dressed. I was a normally put-together person, but some mornings I didn't want to fix my hair or put on my face. For no particular reason, some days were easier than others. I continued my therapy sessions.

I began to say the words, "failed Frozen Embryo Transfer," when talking to my Inner Circle and doctors during appointments. Saying those words really solidified what I still believed was my ultimate failure. The more I talked about it, the more I felt the gravity of my loss was still prevalent.

As a teacher, I had an extended Winter Break. I dreaded the time off. Work provided me with a daily routine and purpose. I was concerned about being alone without that routine. Jim and I came up with a plan that I would reach out to friends and schedule outings or activities with them to make sure I interacted with others instead of wallowing. We also realized that I needed down time to continue processing my emotions and depression.

I spent Christmas Eve at my parents' house assembling our annual Christmas cookie trays. I met Brandon for lunch before returning to my parents' house for Christmas Eve dinner. I considered going to church, but I was too weepy.

Christmas Day was disastrous. I arrived at my parents' house exhausted from a bout of early-morning vomiting. My nerves had gotten the better of me. I stormed out of my parents' house after arguing with my sister. Eventually, I returned to open gifts and eat dinner. Then, I went home.

During the rest of my Winter Break, I kept to the plan of scheduling time with others and down time for myself. I met with friends for lunch. I hosted a friend from out of town. I treated myself to a manicure and a massage. I attended a friend's dinner party, where she'd kept the guest list a surprise. I saw people I'd not seen in over a year and met some new faces, one of whom became my writing partner/ mentor. I took my nephew and his crew bowling. I celebrated New Year's Eve with friends in a family setting. I ordered new bedroom furniture and put the old furniture online for sale. A friend cooked dinner for me.

When classes resumed in January, I was more rested and could tackle each day more efficiently. By mid-January, I had the rest of my lessons planned and all necessary materials sent to be copied by our in-house copy center. I began attending an exercise class through the local community college. I resumed belly dance classes and accepted an invitation to perform with the class in March.

I reached out to friends, family, and colleagues to let them know, in general terms, that I had a rough 2015 and was looking forward to changing my traffic pattern in the New Year. I asked that if they were doing anything fun or out of my comfort zone to think about including me. I asked if they knew any interesting people for me to meet. I needed to expand my circle. Some responses were immediate. A colleague stopped by my classroom the next week, and we agreed to go for lunch during a professional development day.

My dear friends, Gina and Paul, gifted me the book *The Secret*, which I'd read many years prior. They'd both recently read it and thought it something I needed to read and put into practice. I re-read it and began to take baby steps to put its principles into practice.

I felt like I was coming out of my isolation and beginning to live again. I'm not going to lie and say everything is better all of the time because it's not. I have almost an equal number of good and bad days. When I have bad days, they're quite bad, though. It's as if my body and emotions store up all of my pain and anger until they need to unload. I don't enjoy those days, because they're extremely intense and full of crying and screaming. However, they're much less frequent than they were initially.

Full acceptance hasn't happened. Rationally, I knew that I would never be a genetic mother. I'd just lost the chance to be a biological mother. Emotionally, I'd not fully accepted that my dream of being a mother was over.

Those closest to me were concerned that I wasn't bouncing back as quickly as I normally did when faced with adversity, but I'd never experienced that degree of pain and loss before. I questioned my faith and God. I hated my body for betraying me and not allowing me the most basic function of being pregnant. I resented others for simply living--for going through their daily lives when I was in such a dark emotional place. I felt abandoned by others as they moved on with their lives. Upon reflection, to say that this journey had broken me was not completely accurate. I was terribly battered.

The aftermath of my failed FET ran the gamut from shock, numbness, and isolation into full-scale grief into something manageable. My sense of loss will always be in my heart, but time is giving me some perspective. Resuming some semblance of a normal routine helped. Committing to physical activities allowed my body to adjust to its new normal. Reaching out to others is something I don't like to do, but it was a blessing to connect and reconnect with those around me. Changing my traffic pattern and adding to my circle challenged me to move forward.

Years prior, after my mother was diagnosed with breast cancer, I told her that she could have fifteen minutes each day to focus on her cancer, anger, sadness or frustration. She could scream, swear, cry or do whatever she needed to do during that solid fifteen minutes. After that, she had to live. I think it was great advice. She occasionally thanks me for giving her that advice. When she reminded of the advice I'd given her, it was hard for me to follow it. My life had been dominated by grief for weeks. That grief dictated my daily activities. Now, I'm trying to set aside a small period each day to mourn my loss, rather than have it dominate my life.

Unadulterated Shame

You've got to trust yourself. Be gentle with yourself.
And listen to yourself.
You're the only person who can get you through this now.
You're the only one who can survive your story,
the only one who can write your future.
All you've got to do, when you're ready, is stand up,
{and begin again.}
Tessa Shaffer

After my failed FET, the feeling of shame returned with a vengeance. Not only did I have physically nothing to show for having my FET, but I also had a vast void in my spirit. There are still days that I feel less than a full woman.

Webster's Online defines shame as:

"A painful emotion caused by consciousness of guilt, shortcoming, or impropriety; a condition of humiliating disgrace or disrepute; something to be regretted."

According to that definition, I met most of the criteria for shame. My emotions had been painful and caused by consciousness of shortcoming. I had a condition of humiliating disgrace. I regretted, and some days still regret, not being able to bear a child.

The devastating loss caused more emotional pain than I ever experienced or thought I could endure. My body's inability to carry a pregnancy was my shortcoming. I, alone, felt the humiliation of feeling less than a woman.

It was easy for those on the outside who told me that my inability to have a child did nothing to diminish my womanhood; however, I felt the complete opposite. What man wants to be with a woman who can't have a child? Who wants to be with a woman who is ashamed of her body? Who wants to be around a woman who can't control her emotions and is prone to uncontrollable emotional outbursts? Who wants to be in the presence of a woman who feels her self-worth obliterated?

Rationally, I knew that those around me said that I was an intelligent woman, who'd always given to those around me. They marveled at how I managed to put on a smile and do my job everyday, without letting my personal turmoil influence on my teaching performance. They're amazed that I'd been at work every day through the withdrawal and the emotional fallout. They said I was a woman who cares about things most people don't. They said I'm a good person. They told me I was beautiful and even sexy. They told me they loved me.

I wasn't ready to accept that what those around me are saying is true. I didn't feel giving or amazing or caring or good. I didn't feel beautiful, and I surely felt anything but sexy.

I guess that's the perplexing thing about shame. Shame is a matter of perception. No one else saw me the way I did then. I put the shame on myself, and only I can work through things to remove it. I didn't know if I could completely rid myself of the shame.

Support

**It is when there is nothing you can say or do to help
that a friend needs you the most.**
Robert Brault

If I can impress upon you one thing and one thing alone, support is essential. I am always mindful of three things my wise friend, Paul, told me. You can't tell another person what they need. You can't tell another person what to think. You can't tell another person how to feel. You can only be there for that person in a non-judgmental capacity.

My ex-fiancé was supportive from the first day of my diagnosis on September 8, 2014, until the end of the relationship. He was on board with whatever decision I made. He held me when I sobbed uncontrollably. He cried with me. He guided me to bed when I couldn't function. He was a rock during one of the most turbulent times in my life.

I think one of the most profound things those around me didn't know and couldn't understand is what I gave up when I ended my engagement. They saw what they perceived to be my extreme anguish as I ended a romantic relationship. No doubt there was emotional anguish, but it was not solely from choosing to end my relationship. What they were not privy to was that I effectively ended my chances at carrying the child of someone I loved. In addition, as I would learn months later, I took myself out of the Egg Donor program, by not having a partner. I mourned that conscious choice for weeks.

My family's support ran the gamut from openness, acceptance, and full support to completely shutting down and ignoring my diagnosis and choices. At a time when I needed unconditional support, understanding, and non-judgmental interactions, I experienced an emotional roller coaster.

When I first learned of my infertility diagnosis, I didn't want to share the news with my family. At the urging of my ex-fiancé, I set up a meeting at my parents' house. I asked my sister to meet me, so I could share the news with both my mother and her at the same time instead of having to repeat it. For her own reasons, my sister couldn't make it. Consequently, I shared the information with my mom, who had downcast eyes and silently wrung her hands throughout my conversation with her. At the end of that conversation, she told me she'd support whatever it was I chose to do.

Later that day, my sister demanded that I tell her my news over the phone. I explained that some information should be shared in person, and this was that type of information. She didn't relent in her insistence. Eventually, I was so tired of being badgered that I told her over the phone. Her immediate reaction was to offer her eggs to me. I thanked her, and I explained that she didn't meet the egg donation criteria.

As I progressed through my months-long diagnostic testing and medical protocols, my family was fairly supportive and respectful when I shared that I was going for various phases of testing. They didn't ask intrusive questions or pry for information. They took my lead.

That changed in May of 2015. After disclosing that I was again single to my team at Magee, I was no longer eligible for the Magee-Women's Hospital of UPMC's Egg Donor program. I also learned that my only remaining option for me was an Embryo Donation program. The same day, my colleague and former roommate came into my classroom before the start of the day to share that she and her husband were expecting their third child and another teacher in her department was expecting her first child. She was sensitive to my needs and wanted me to hear the news from her directly. I hugged her crying; I was happy for her, but it devastated me to know someone else was pregnant when I wasn't.

That afternoon, I spoke with my mother and explained the situation. More importantly, I expressed how sad I was about being told I could physically maintain a pregnancy, but my fertility practice at

Magee did not offer a Donor-Donor program, where I could "outsource eggs and sperm." Her response was to "get a thicker skin." Our relationship wasn't the same after that day.

I emotionally crumbled at work that day. That afternoon, I walked through the hallway of my school in shock. Somehow I made it back to my classroom before the uncontrollable sobbing came. Two of my colleagues, Rich and Doug, sat with me in my darkened classroom, sitting by my side as I rocked back and forth unable to lift my head from my hands. Both offered to drive me home from work. Eventually they requested that administration have another teacher cover my last class of the day. No questions were asked. They did what they knew how to do; they protected and took care of me.

That evening, when I told my sister that news, she reiterated her egg offer. I thanked her and declined, as she didn't meet the criteria. As much as I impressed my desire to conceive, carry, and deliver a child, she didn't seem to understand that I wanted the total pregnancy experience.

From that point on, I hesitated to share any news with my family regarding my infertility treatment for fear of judgment and additional hurt. I cut most ties with my mother for the majority of the summer of 2015. I didn't discuss anything of a personal medical nature with either her or my sister.

Then, the most remarkable thing happened, something I chose to keep private from my family until I'd thoroughly researched all aspects and the final arrangements had been made. I was presented with the miraculous opportunity of having a genetically healthy, male embryo transferred into me via a Frozen Embryo Transfer (FET).

In October of 2015, when it came time to share the news of my impending FET in Cancun, I waited until about three weeks before I was to leave. I was in the final phase of my pre-FET medical protocol. My travel arrangements were confirmed, and I'd submitted my leave paperwork from work, before I shared my story with my family.

I called a family meeting at my house, inviting my parents and my sister. My parents came at the appointed time, but my sister chose not to. I prepared folders of medical, travel, and other pertinent information. (Those of you who know me even moderately well should be chuckling at that.) I shared my story and travel plans. To my surprise and delight, my parents were fully supportive. In fact, my mother, who was seventy-five at the time, applied for an expedited renewed passport to travel with me. Although I appreciated her effort, there would have been no way I would have let her go with me. The travel alone would have been physically impossible for her.

My sister was another story. I tried to persuade her to join us for the family meeting. She insisted on having the conversation over the phone, at swim team practice, or in the car the next night outside of a dance studio. I told her wanted to share this exciting news in person.

She didn't see the need to do that. She called our parents for my news. After speaking with our parents, she was told that it was my information to share, not theirs. Surprisingly, she rang my doorbell just before 9:00 the night of the family meeting, as I was getting ready for bed.

I welcomed her into my living room, grabbed an information folder for her, and began my story. She interrogated me with rapid-fire questions while she checked her mobile phone. When I sensed the conversation wasn't going well, I told her I simply needed her support. She looked at me and said, "I'll have to think about that," stood up, and headed for the front door. Barely three minutes had elapsed since her arrival. Since I'm extremely close with my niece and nephew, I wanted them to know I was leaving for a short while, and I asked my sister if I could tell my niece and nephew that I was going on a vacation, with no other details. I thought that would proactively alleviate any issues or questions from them.

Her response was, "Give me some credit." Then she got in her car and drove away.

I didn't and don't understand her complete disregard toward my feelings and my decision. I can't say we were particularly close growing up, but I guess I expected some--any--empathy from her. I received none. I expected to be respected. I wasn't. In the months since that failed conversation, my sister did not ask me another question about my decision or wish me well. I've rarely felt the deep pain inflicted on me by my sister.

My sister didn't acknowledge anything about my trip other than a few text messages when I was gone, one of which was to inform me that she told my niece and nephew that I needed a vacation and took a trip to Mexico. The only question she asked about the reason for my trip was to ask if "I was done medically." Not, "How are you doing?" Not, "Was the transfer successful?" Not, "I hope you're okay." It was and continued to be a whole lot of nothing.

I needed her to show compassion toward me. I needed her to respect my decision, even if she didn't understand or agree with it. I needed her to at least acknowledge that I was taking the biggest risk and undergoing the most important medical procedure of my life. She didn't even tell me goodbye before I left. There was a total disconnect.

On my way to Cancun, I sat on a layover in Houston. I struck up a conversation with a couple from New Jersey who were headed to a resort in Cancun during their kids' fall break. When the husband asked why I was traveling, I told them I was going to Cancun to try to become pregnant. After the look on his face and an awkward chuckle at how he thought I was going to achieve that goal, his wife asked if I was going to a clinic. I gave them the abbreviated version of the story. They were both so accepting of my news and seemed genuine when they wished me well.

I received more compassion from complete strangers in the Houston Airport than my own sister. It's unconscionable. Since my return from Cancun, my sister simply said that she guessed I'd been through a lot.

After I arrived in Cancun, my mother offered support through emails and the three phone calls I made Stateside. She was concerned about my safety, my medical care, and my emotional state. I expressed that I was mostly bored but that everything was going according to plan. As a family support system, mine made my journey somewhat more stressful.

Fortunately, I had an amazing group of friends, my Inner Circle, as I called them. Throughout my journey, my Inner Circle stood by me despite their initial shock, skepticism, and tough love. They took in overwhelming amounts of information. They witnessed emotional meltdowns. They wrestled with their own ethical and moral questions regarding my decision. They honestly voiced their concerns, keeping my well-being as the priority. They talked me down when I needed grounding. They unconditionally supported and loved me in spite of it all. I love each and every one of you and can never repay your kindness.

My Inner Circle--Gina, Paul, Beth, Teri, Debbie, Megan, Rosemary, Diane, and Carl, some who have children and some who don't have children, asked pertinent and pointed questions about my motivation in wanting to pursue motherhood in my forties. They were concerned about my physical health and more importantly about my emotional well-being. They let me cry when I needed to cry, live when I needed to live, and be when I needed to be. They didn't intrude when I needed time to process information and emotions.

My lifelong friend, Tom, and I had many Face Time conversations from my earliest investigation to my journey toward motherhood in Cancun. From his home base in Paris, or wherever he traveled for business, Tom was my sounding board. He listened when I vented or second-guessed myself. He doled out the tough love when I needed it. Tom knew me better than almost anyone, and he told me what I needed, not necessarily what I wanted to hear. I knew he was always only a few clicks of the mouse away. I missed him being with me in person. I knew I had Tom's unconditional love and support.

My friend and confidante, Brandon, stood by me in the States. Although Brandon knew of my desire to be a mother, I'd not shared all of the summer time developments with him. I was afraid of telling him about the gift that was being given to me because I thought he would turn his back on me. Instead, he comforted me and told me that things would be okay. It was the true testament of our friendship. He volunteered to bring me ice cream for any cravings and hold me when I cried from pregnancy hormones. His standard statement was, "You've got this, and I've got you."

Brandon drove me home from the airport when I arrived home. I believe he wanted me to be pregnant almost as much as I did. He was the first person I told about the failed FET. If it couldn't have been Tom, I was thankful it was Brandon.

I couldn't have asked for better colleagues than the handful with whom I shared my story. I approached my teaching partner and then union president, Doug, early on in my initial decision for professional feedback about potential ramifications of teaching and single motherhood. I was proud to call these colleagues my friends. I shared my story with some of them when I was in tearful states at various times throughout my journey.

Even if they didn't agree with my decision, my colleagues all respected my decision and supported me in a variety of individualized ways. Some days, they walked into my room before classes to find me staring off into the room or already dissolving into tears. On those days, they closed the door and sometimes just held me until I regained my composure. On other days, they shut the door, so I could take the time to myself. They sent periodic text messages to check on me when I was having a rough day, a string of rough days, or when I was awaiting my FET in Cancun. They stood by me in discussions with Human Resources. They prayed for me. Most of all, they all maintained my confidence and ensured my privacy.

When I returned from Cancun, it was brought to my attention that a few colleagues were gossiping about my absence. Somehow, the private nature of my trip had become water cooler gossip for some. They knew specific details that I shared with so few others. My trusted colleagues deflected the gossip, so I wouldn't have to deal with it. I'm grateful to them for that. It's not often that I felt I could trust anyone with such sensitive and private information.

For those who participated in such gossip, you increased my stress level at a time when I was supposed to maintain a stress-free existence. Any time I'd heard a rumor about a colleague, I approached that colleague privately in person to express my concern. I guess I expected the same in kind. Your behavior was cruel and unacceptable, and to my discredit, I allowed your behavior to negatively impact me.

My teammates and many other colleagues with whom I didn't share my journey knew something was amiss. However, they let me be. They didn't ask questions, merely offered a quiet smile or head nod. There was no way for them to know how much their unintentional support meant to me.

I'd had the fortune to connect with a fantastic therapist, the late James Donnelly. He's the first therapist, with whom I'd worked, who offered honest, practical advice. He reminded me that I was the only one to whom I had to answer. Jim was not only empathetic but also offered sound advice to help me through my infertility diagnosis, break up, and failed FET.

Despite all of the support I had and continue to have, it felt like the pain, anguish, and grief would never diminish. I will probably struggle with my emotions for quite some time. I can't imagine how different things would be if I didn't have the support I did. To this day, I continue to surround myself with those who continue to support me and leave those who drain me behind.

Things That Would Have Been Nice to Know

Life isn't about how comfortable I can be.
It is about learning how to get comfortable
with being uncomfortable.
Heather Gillis

When I began my journey toward motherhood, I was a novice when it came to understanding fertility. I looked online for resources and blogs to provide me with general information. I asked my Egg Ladies if they could coordinate a meeting or conversation with another single woman going through the same experience. I looked for locally-based and online support groups.

Much to my surprise, I found very little information about fertility in general and a single woman facing my unique challenges in particular. I found very little, and that which I did find didn't really pertain to my situation. I wish there had been something, anything, for me to read or a group with whom I could ask questions and share, but I could find very little information anywhere.

In retrospect, I wanted and needed to know so much more than I did at the time. I learned as I went, but I was frustrated by my relative lack of knowledge, the slow pace, and my inability to control the process. I had no idea what I was about to experience and very little guidance to help me prepare for it.

I wish I had known how arduous the diagnostic process would be. My fertility team at Magee provided me with a checklist of tests and appointments needed for their Egg Donor program, but they didn't include information about side effects of the various protocols or begin to touch upon the emotional component. It would be an incredibly grueling process both physically and emotionally.

The physical changes alone were not at all what I was prepared for or expected. The hormonal treatment for the mock cycles caused immediate physical changes in my body. The cycles of estrogen caused weight gain and an increase in breast size. I developed adult acne. Emotionally, during that time, I was in a constant state of irritability and short-temperedness. Imagine being in a PMS state for ten days, two weeks, or four weeks at a time with sometimes less than a week of recovery time between cycles. I was not a pleasant woman to be around.

Once I was into my pre-FET phase, the increase in progesterone caused extreme breast tenderness and utter exhaustion. The latter was a plus for me, as I didn't sleep but for a few hours a night. I actually slept consistently for a short time. My midsection became thicker, and my already tight clothes became tighter. During my FET protocol, I changed progesterone prescriptions to avoid anaphylactic symptoms. The change in brand resulted in additional breast tenderness and mild nausea.

After my failed FET, I was advised to stop taking all of my medications. I unknowingly began withdrawing from them. Had I known how bad that would be, I would have weaned myself off of them. I lost nine pounds from my petite frame in less than three weeks. It was as though I was detoxing from narcotics or psychiatric drugs.

I needed guidance to communicate with my family and friends. I knew of no one in my circle with whom I could speak about a failed FET. Although some of my friends had suffered and mourned miscarriages, mine was a different type of mourning. Some of my friends had experienced infertility and undergone a variety of treatments, but they all became pregnant and carried pregnancies to term. It's strange as I reflect, because until I shared my story with them, I didn't know that many of them had suffered from infertility.

Here is what I think a woman should know when considering alternate means to conceive a child. Consider them my words from my experience and the school of hard knocks. Reducing and managing stress is paramount to physical and emotional health. This is true for everyone, not just women navigating infertility. I practiced daily yoga meditation and try to maintain an exercise program. I journal. I keep busy.

Having a support system is absolutely necessary, so you have to ask for and accept support in any and all forms. You can only isolate yourself for so long. Recognizing that even if people around you may not know what to say or how to say it, they love and support you in their own way. Some may convey tough love in conversations. Others may drop off a small bouquet of flowers or send a "thinking of you" card. It's important to remember that most people don't know how to help; they just want to help. Do your best to graciously accept their efforts.

Emotions are significantly impacted by hormonal treatments. You can only control emotions to a point before they have to come out. At one point, mine boiled over in a local restaurant, when I began crying after receiving an unrelated and insignificant text message. I looked at a dividing mirror in the restaurant and wondered who the crying woman was. Then I realized the reflection in the mirror was mine. Once the tears started, they didn't stop, and I excused myself to the ladies room until I regained my composure. The emotions have to come out; although, you can't always control when and where that will happen.

Coming off of high doses of hormonal medications cold turkey, as I said, is similar to withdrawing from narcotics or anti-anxiety medications. In my experience, I lost nine pounds in less than a month from day and night sweats, nausea, vomiting, diarrhea, and not wanting to eat. I wish I had known, as I now do that I could have been weaned in a controlled manner to avoid the body aches and irritability that accompanied the other symptoms. Looking back, I probably should have probably consulted my Primary Care Physician or OBGYN for an assessment and possible help.

Request Obstetric (OB) ultrasound technicians so that your many transvaginal ultrasounds are as "pleasant" as possible. There is a distinct difference in ultrasound technicians.   OB ultrasound technicians, in my experience, have a defter and gentler technique than general ultrasound technicians.

Listen to your body and communicate your needs clearly to medical staff with whom you come into contact. In my case, I always let my phlebotomist know very specific details before he or she applied the tourniquet to my arm. My left arm had better veins for a multiple-vial blood draw. Sometimes a pediatric needle was the best option. Even though I've had blood drawn countless times, when I stopped talking with the person who was drawing my blood, I was not far from fainting. Communicating helped my phlebotomists prepare for those times when I came close to hitting the deck.

Advocate for yourself. Something I tell my students is that no question is unintelligent. Write down and ask your medical team any and all questions you have. Write down and repeat the answers you're given to confirm that the information communicated back to you is accurate. Be proactive with your insurance company and persistent if and when you need to follow up to receive the answers given to you. Document every conversation with dates, times, the name of the person who takes your call and a summary of the information given to you, so you can refer to it if needed at a later time.

The two most important things I've learned can really serve anyone in any situation. They're sometimes hard to recall and apply though. First, be kind to yourself. Take time out of each day to focus on the blessings in your life. Whether you go for a walk, hit a punching bag, or cook a fantastic meal, do something to nurture yourself every day. Finally, no one has the right to judge you for your decisions. Only you walk your journey. Whether or not you have a partner in your life, it's your body, your emotional state, and ultimately your decision.

Collateral Damage of Healthcare Giants

**People at war with themselves will always cause
collateral damage
in the lives of those around them.
John Mark Green**

During the time I walked my fertility journey, Western Pennsylvania was in an awkward situation when it came to health insurance. The University of Pittsburgh Medical Center (UPMC) and Highmark are the two regional healthcare giants. On December 31, 2014, the two healthcare systems "divorced," for lack of a better description. There was a Consent Decree, which stated that subscribers could see their doctors, even if those doctors were from the opposing insurer, as long as they had been seen within the 2014 calendar year and/or had a prior condition that required continuity of care. Only then, would a subscriber be given the privilege of staying with that doctor through the calendar year 2015.

I'm a public school teacher. In Western Pennsylvania, most school districts are members of a health care consortium that procures health insurance for over 30,000 subscribers, plus their family members. Through my employer and the Consortium, Highmark is the only option other than paying out-of-pocket for another insurer.

As of December 31, 2014, UPMC and Highmark subscribers could no longer use UPMC's doctors and/or medical facilities at in-network cost unless it was an Emergency Department visit, ongoing oncology care, or care for a prior condition with the UPMC doctor consenting to continue treating the patient.

I'd inquired with one of my health care consortium's board members, who was a teacher in my school district, as well as my school district's benefits coordinator. I was advised to be proactive in the event that UPMC and Highmark would not come to an agreement by the end of 2014.

As a result of this insurance split, my OBGYN practice of more than two decades was not be able to keep me as a patient at in-network rates. I subsequently filed a complaint against the OBGYN's office with the Pennsylvania State Attorney General's Office in November of 2014, because I believed the office was in violation of the Consent Decree, as I was being treated for an ongoing medical condition.

I spent the next several weeks working with Highmark, in the event that there was no settlement between the health care giants, to get references for new OBGYN practices. I had specific criteria, as I was going to continue my fertility journey. While I still maintained my fertility doctor at UPMC, all of my other gynecological and general health care had to be coordinated through Highmark physicians and facilities in order to receive covered care.

In this era of managed health care, I think it's rare to have a solid, respectful, long-term, professional relationship with any physician. Dr. Simmonds was one of those old-fashioned doctors who truly listened to his patients' concerns and made his own follow-up calls after office hours. Over the last twenty plus years, he provided not only clinical and diagnostic services to me, but he was a sounding board for me and calmed me down when problems occurred. He walked me through two separate potential breast cancer "scares," including biopsies, and ongoing health issues. Regardless of which office he saw patients on any given day, he always returned my calls personally between patients or after office hours.

In an attempt to stay with Dr. Simmonds, I made a personal plea in my last appointment, on November 24, 2014, as I was advised to do to be able to continue my care with that practice. Dr. Simmonds told me that the decision had been made, and it wasn't his decision to make. I began to cry when he told me that. He hugged me as I cried, handed me a tissue and left the examination room. I dissolved and left the office in tears.

That December during my Christmas Break, I interviewed OBGYN practices--something that I found is rarely done--to see which would be the best fit for me. I was fortunate to have found a practice that sees a gamut of patients from teens to women of advanced maternal age, that does on-call service within its own practice, and that handles fertility patients. I was forced to seek out new imaging and diagnostic centers. I requested that my medical records be sent from UPMC doctors to my new ones.

What UPMC and Highmark lost complete sight of, if they ever had sight of it in the first place, is that their subscribers were collateral damage. We were the ones who had to find new physicians. We were the ones who had to go for medical tests in new labs and facilities. We were the ones who had to request medical records that often didn't show up at the new doctor's office until after a new-patient appointment. We were the faceless names who are so unnecessarily disregarded by two insurance companies that were in a giant tug of war.

As an aside, the Attorney General's Office followed up with me in a phone call six months after I submitted my complaint. Within a week of that phone call, UPMC directors called to tell me that I could still see my former OBGYN. Although that was a huge victory for me, it was too little, way too late.

At a critical time when my stress level should have been as low as possible, the situation between these two health care giants negatively impacted me. For weeks on end, I spent my lunch and planning periods and countless hours after work on the telephone with both UPMC and Highmark. I tried to sort out the current or "right" interpretation of the Consent Decree, which neither insurer seemed to have. I spoke to various medical practices to see if they were taking new patients. I set up interviews with medical practices. I waded through the insurance appeals process when procedures weren't fully covered. I asked questions of everyone with whom I spoke. It seemed like neither UPMC nor Highmark had quite the same story.

Although it seemed like an exercise in futility, I persisted for months, all the while continuing to complete items on The Checklist. In the end, I am ecstatic with my new OBGYN practice.

The bottom line is that no one should have to experience this level of blatant disrespect and disregard. Shame on both UPMC and Highmark for putting their subscribers in such a difficult position.

Happy Un-Mother's Day

We shall draw from the heart of suffering itself
the means of inspiration and survival.
Winston Churchill

Despite the progress I'd made, Mother's Day 2016 was exceptionally difficult. My sister still didn't seem to understand or want to understand my decision to have an embryo transfer. I was invited to her house for a cookout and ordered to bring dessert. When I explained that I wasn't sure how I would feel and not to count on me to attend, I was slightly brow beaten, but I stood my ground.

On Mother's Day morning, my nephew and I participated in Pittsburgh's annual Susan G. Komen Race for the Cure. We walked hand-in-hand from vendor to vendor and table to table, loving on each other. I received a number of "Happy Mother's Days" from volunteers and strangers. I graciously nodded through a forced smile and gritted teeth. I guess it was completely plausible that he could be my son, but I hadn't prepared myself for the sentiments or emotional reactions of the day.

By the time we returned to his house, I was already teetering on the edge of a good or ugly crying fit. When I arrived at my house, I sat in silence to process what the morning had presented. Then, I began "keeping busy." I texted Mother's Day wishes to my friends. I scrubbed my house from top to bottom. I made wedding soup and ham stock. I folded laundry and ironed clothes. I washed my bedclothes and remade the bed. Dinner was a double-scoop ice cream sundae with caramel and marshmallow toppings.

Throughout the day, my new boyfriend and I texted, as he was out of town. We spoke in the early evening, and he listened as I vented. It was reassuring to know he cared, even if he didn't fully understand the emotions I was experiencing. There was a lot more I wanted and needed to share with him about my emotions, but I wanted to do that in person.

My parents stopped by after the cookout at my sister's house. I gave my mom her Mother's Day card and a hanging basket. They gave me a sunflower plant to let me know they were thinking of me. That support went a long way to helping me through the challenging day.

Moving Forward

**The art of living lies less in eliminating our troubles
than in growing with them.
Bernard M. Baruch**

As I look back, it had been well over a month since I attempted to write anything new since the previous chapter. I think I burned myself out emotionally by reliving such recent, raw memories each time I accessed my flash drive. Not only had I gone through the physical recovery of not being pregnant and having my body begin to regulate itself hormonally after nearly a year of treatments and protocols, but I'd also undergone an uncontrollable upheaval and subsequent growth in my emotional stability from the disappointment and grief I suffered.

As I continued to work through my roller coaster of physical and emotional changes in the weeks and months since my failed embryo transfer, I learned more than I imagined about myself and those around me. I was pushed to the emotional brink and came close to destruction. However, I pulled myself out of bed every single day, even after sometimes having no recollection of how I got into bed the previous night. I allowed tears to flow uncontrollably whenever and wherever they chose to surface. I accepted that crying and asking for help were signs of strength, not weakness. I clawed my way out of my self-imposed isolation and began to reconnect with my Inner Circle, my family, and people around me.

I began to let go of the stress associated with the last two years. My desire to cook returned, and I began eating regularly. I gained back a couple of the pounds I lost. When I was up to it, I made my way to the end of my street and back, a leisurely, hilly, two-mile walk. I completed my outdoor Spring chores to get my yard looking decent. I even went clothes shopping for the first time in almost a year. While I still had issues with how my body had changed, I didn't completely shy away from mirrors.

Since I function well with a routine, I began to schedule things for myself. Once something is entered into my phone's calendar, I follow through with it. Subsequently, I resumed belly dance classes and periodic yoga workshops. I met friends for dinner, drinks, and coffee. I started dating again.

The majority of those around me were amazingly supportive. Friends and family members checked on me unobtrusively via text and email. I received periodic cards of support. Colleagues who knew my story poked their heads into my classroom to say a quick hello or give me a hug.

I started to share my story with a handful of people other than those who had maintained my confidence. After the initial shock and disbelief wore off, I found people to be supportive. Their concern was for me and how I was doing. Sharing with more people incrementally lessened my burden and sadness, and it let me feel like I was living a little more each day. That wasn't to say that some days weren't much more challenging to navigate than others, but those days became fewer and less emotionally-intense and draining.

I was still navigating Kubler-Ross's stages and was moving toward acceptance. I accepted that my body cannot create a life and probably never could. Some days I wondered that if I'd known about my infertility diagnosis years ago, I would have attempted IVF or an embryo transfer at an earlier age. I still struggled with the knowledge that there was the possibility that I could undergo a successful embryo transfer and sustain a healthy pregnancy to term. I just didn't know if I could undergo the physical withdrawal and emotional toll with another failed attempt. What I experienced was so brutal. I knew I still had significant work to do to fully and finally accept all aspects of losing my dream of motherhood.

For many people, tattoos mark life-changing events or the passage of time. For others, tattoos are a permanent tribute or celebration of someone or something. Sometimes tattoos are impulsive and frivolous.

I have two in celebration and two more frivolous. After some thought, I decided to tell the story of my fertility journey, in ink.

In January of 2016, in an effort to help me move forward in my healing process, I contacted the tattoo shop where my longtime tattoo artist, Jim, worked. I wanted him to design a tattoo that symbolized my journey, specifically my failed embryo transfer. I provided him with the abbreviated version of my story and emailed images of the conjoined heart necklace I'd purchased in Cancun. I asked him to incorporate praying hands or angel wings, something to mark the passing of my dream of biological motherhood. I gave Jim total creative license. Then, I waited three months for my appointment.

I knew "tattoo day" would be emotional. Although my new boyfriend wasn't able to join me, he offered his support. I drove alone to my session, which in the end was fitting. I'd started this journey on my own nearly two years prior; this was something that I needed to do on my own. I wasn't sure how I would react seeing Jim's design or how I'd sit through my session; however, I knew that this was a necessary step for me to begin really letting go.

I didn't see the finished design until the day of my session, but I trusted Jim artistically and as someone who understood the significance of what I wanted. When I arrived at Mantis Tattoo on May 3, 2016, I was anxiously excited. When Jim showed me his initial design, I became a little teary-eyed. Jim told me not to cry. I knew that he was in tune with me. His design was beyond what I had envisioned.

He used the image of the conjoined hearts from my necklace as the focal point of the tattoo. He wrapped an angel's wing on the right side of the larger heart, gently caressing it and extended the other wing upward. The image flowed beautifully to the heavens above. Initially, I'd thought that black and gray was the way to go, and Jim agreed.

After setting up his station and creating the stencil, Jim was ready to begin. I chose to have the tattoo placed on my right side and ribs. I thought it would be my most painful tattoo to date, and I was absolutely correct in that prediction. I don't have a lot of fat on my side flank and ribs, so with each passing of the tattoo machine, I experienced a moderate to high level of hot, sharp, cutting pain. Usually, after a few minutes into a tattoo, endorphins kick in, and there is a "high" or sense of euphoria. I didn't experience that "high" with this tattoo. Jim and I chatted, catching up on the past couple of years about kids, exes, and life. When the pain surged, I became quiet. Each time Jim worked toward or on my ribs, I cringed on the inside. Deep breathing helped some, but at times, it felt like he was pounding hot little nails into my right breast. My nerve endings were on fire.

We took a short break after about forty minutes in. Overall, I stayed as still as possible for nearly an hour while Jim worked his magic. When Jim was sufficiently satisfied with his efforts, he invited me to look into the mirror for the first time.

Through the droplets of blood, I saw a gorgeous piece of artwork that symbolically told the most significant and heartbreaking part of my story. In the tattoo, I saw my August within me, me holding him before sending him on, and him ascending to Heaven. While I didn't cry, Jim put his arms around my shoulders, hugging me. He wiped down the tattoo, bandaged me, and sent me on my way. I'm blessed to have such an empathetic man and gifted artist to create this lasting tribute.

I drove home, my side throbbing, feeling content with what I'd done that evening. I thought I'd cry as a release from months of grief, but I didn't. My boyfriend offered to take me to dinner when I returned home. I appreciated his offer, but I'd eaten prior to my session. We went to a local watering hole, so he could eat. We talked about my evening. Then, he held me that night. I was grateful to be able to share that part of my journey with him.

As my tattoo healed, a beautiful softness emerged. There were subtle shades of gray filling in the clear lines around the hearts. It's feminine and strong, like I've become.

Most of those who knew my story saw what I saw. They offered their support and approval. Others saw the tattoo as two hearts and angel wings assuming they had something to do with love and death, but they didn't understand the deeper symbolism or my motivation for the tattoo.

At some point, perhaps after reading this book, they'll understand why I chose to use it as the image on the cover.

Love Letters

**I never knew until that moment how bad it could hurt
to lose something you never really had.
From the television show *The Wonder Years***

While in Cancun, awaiting my Frozen Embryo Transfer, I began writing a series of letters to my embryo, whom I named August, after the month in which he came into being. Ironically, had I become pregnant, he would have been born in August as well. I thought it was important for him to know of the last leg of my journey to meet him. I'd hoped to share these letters with him some day.

November 2, 2015
Dear Baby August,

Yesterday, I took another step in my journey to meet you. I flew from my home in Pittsburgh, Pennsylvania to Cancun by way of Houston, Texas. It was a long and tiring day of travel, but when I finally made it through Immigration and Customs, I knew I was one step closer to meeting you.

Jorge, my driver, was waiting for me and delivered me safely to my hotel. I unpacked and had what I hope to be my last glass of wine for a very long time. Strangely, I slept well in my unfamiliar bed.

This morning, Jorge drove me to meet with the staff at the Fertility Center Cancun. My body has responded well to the medical protocol I began weeks ago. I'm ready for you to join me. I'm excited and a little anxious and scared about what's to come. I guess that's true of any mother-to-be.

However, I think it's more so in my case. I've waited such a long time for this opportunity. I've done everything I could physically do to make sure I'm as healthy as I can be. I've taken months of medication, had more tests than I can count and struggled through more emotional outbursts than I care to recall. It's all come down to this. In five, short days, I could be your Mommy.

Saturday seems so far away right now. You'll learn soon enough that I like to be busy. Actually, I don't do "down time" very well. Maybe that's the lesson for me this week, to be patient. My job now is to relax and make sure my body is well-rested for you.

Love, Mom

November 5, 2015
Dear Baby August,

Today I wrote quite a bit of my story, so that other women who want to be moms don't get discouraged. Rather, I hope that they're inspired to stick with their dream of becoming moms. Some day, I want to share my, our, whole story with you and the world.

I feel like I've fought so hard to be your Mom. There have been many obstacles in my journey, but they've all been worth it. In two short days, we'll meet each other.

There are so many people who want to meet you. Your grandparents are excited to meet you. I think once your cousins know, they won't be able to wait to meet you, help to take care of you, and teach you everything they know. You'll love Momoko. She's a caring, giving, loving, intelligent young lady. Kiyoshi is sensitive, loving, and so smart. He'll teach you about doing "boy things." You're going to have so many "aunts and uncles" who will help you to be a strong, incredible man.

Love, Mom

November 6, 2015
Dear Baby August,

Today I feel so strong. I worked with a man named Ricardo. He performed laser acupuncture on me. It was designed to clear any energy blocks in my body and to help further prepare my body for you tomorrow.

Ricardo assessed my energy and my chakras throughout the session. I brought a lot of oxygen into my system and felt relaxed and lighter when he was finished. By the end of the session, I was almost rid of the "traveler's bark," the annoying cough I get when I travel. I'll work with him again tomorrow, after I meet you.

I feel a sense of calmness. I feel balanced in every way.

Love, Mom

November 7, 2015
Dear Baby August,

Today, I met you for the first time. Dr. Ortiz introduced us to each other just after noon, in Cancun, Mexico. When I saw you inside my belly, I cried tears of joy. You're so tiny, but you're very healthy.

I will do everything in my power to meet you in person. I met with Ricardo for another acupuncture session to keep my body relaxed and my energy strong and balanced. He's very excited for us and wants updated along the way. I ate a decent lunch before trying to nap. I ended up resting rather than napping though.

You'll learn soon enough that I like to be busy, sometimes too busy. You're already helping me to be more present and to take care of myself even better than before.

Love, Mom

November 9, 2015
Dear Baby August,

You took your first plane ride today when we left Cancun for Atlanta.
I feel strong today. I chuckled to myself when I filled out my Customs
form on the airplane. I declared the souvenirs I bought for your
cousins. I didn't "declare" you, because there wasn't an appropriate
place on the form to do so. The layover in Atlanta was long, and I
couldn't wait to get home to rest, to have you home safely.

Brandon picked us up from the Pittsburgh Airport and drove us
home. I think he was excited to see me and can't wait to meet you too.

Welcome home, August.

Love, Mom

November 17, 2015
Dearest August,

Today, the doctors told me that I'm not pregnant. I'm so sad that I
won't ever get to meet you in person. I don't know what went wrong.
I wanted to take care of you so badly. I wanted to watch my belly grow.
I wanted to see your sweet face. I just wanted to love you.

Love, Mom